The Law School Admission Council (LSAC) is a nonprofit corporation that provides unique, state-of-the-art admission products and services to ease the admission process for law schools and their applicants worldwide. Currently, 221 law schools in the United States, Canada, and Australia are members of the Council and benefit from LSAC's services.

LSAC fees, policies, and procedures relating to, but not limited to, test registration, test administration, test score reporting, misconduct and irregularities, Credential Assembly Service (CAS), and other matters may change without notice at any time. Up-to-date LSAC policies and procedures are available at LSAC.org.

ISBN-13: 978-0-9996580-1-7

Print number
10 9 8 7 6 5 4 3 2 1

TABLE OF CONTENTS

INTRODUCTION TO THE LSAT

The Law School Admission Test is a half-day standardized test required for admission to all ABA-approved law schools, most Canadian law schools, and many other law schools. It consists of five 35-minute sections of multiple-choice questions. Four of the five sections contribute to the test taker's score. These sections include one Reading Comprehension section, one Analytical Reasoning section, and two Logical Reasoning sections. The unscored section, commonly referred to as the variable section, typically is used to pretest new test questions or to preequate new test forms. The placement of this section in the LSAT will vary. A 35-minute writing sample is administered at the end of the test. The writing sample is not scored by LSAC, but copies are sent to all law schools to which you apply. The score scale for the LSAT is 120 to 180.

The LSAT is designed to measure skills considered essential for success in law school: the reading and comprehension of complex texts with accuracy and insight; the organization and management of information and the ability to draw reasonable inferences from it; the ability to think critically; and the analysis and evaluation of the reasoning and arguments of others.

The LSAT provides a standard measure of acquired reading and verbal reasoning skills that law schools can use as one of several factors in assessing applicants.

For up-to-date information about LSAC's services, go to our website, LSAC.org.

SCORING

Your LSAT score is based on the number of questions you answer correctly (the raw score). There is no deduction for incorrect answers, and all questions count equally. In other words, there is no penalty for guessing.

Test Score Accuracy—Reliability and Standard Error of Measurement

Candidates perform at different levels on different occasions for reasons quite unrelated to the characteristics of a test itself. The accuracy of test scores is best described by the use of two related statistical terms: reliability and standard error of measurement.

Reliability is a measure of how consistently a test measures the skills being assessed. The higher the reliability coefficient for a test, the more certain we can be that test takers would get very similar scores if they took the test again.

LSAC reports an internal consistency measure of reliability for every test form. Reliability can vary from 0.00 to 1.00, and a test with no measurement error would have a reliability coefficient of 1.00 (never attained in practice). Reliability

coefficients for past LSAT forms have ranged from .90 to .95, indicating a high degree of consistency for these tests. LSAC expects the reliability of the LSAT to continue to fall within the same range.

LSAC also reports the amount of measurement error associated with each test form, a concept known as the standard error of measurement (SEM). The SEM, which is usually about 2.6 points, indicates how close a test taker's observed score is likely to be to his or her true score. True scores are theoretical scores that would be obtained from perfectly reliable tests with no measurement error—scores never known in practice.

Score bands, or ranges of scores that contain a test taker's true score a certain percentage of the time, can be derived using the SEM. LSAT score bands are constructed by adding and subtracting the (rounded) SEM to and from an actual LSAT score (e.g., the LSAT score, plus or minus 3 points). Scores near 120 or 180 have asymmetrical bands. Score bands constructed in this manner will contain an individual's true score approximately 68 percent of the time.

Measurement error also must be taken into account when comparing LSAT scores of two test takers. It is likely that small differences in scores are due to measurement error rather than to meaningful differences in ability. The standard error of score differences provides some guidance as to the importance of differences between two scores. The standard error of score differences is approximately 1.4 times larger than the standard error of measurement for the individual scores.

Thus, a test score should be regarded as a useful but approximate measure of a test taker's abilities as measured by the test, not as an exact determination of his or her abilities. LSAC encourages law schools to examine the range of scores within the interval that probably contains the test taker's true score (e.g., the test taker's score band) rather than solely interpret the reported score alone.

Adjustments for Variation in Test Difficulty

All test forms of the LSAT reported on the same score scale are designed to measure the same abilities, but one test form may be slightly easier or more difficult than another. The scores from different test forms are made comparable through a statistical procedure known as equating. As a result of equating, a given scaled score earned on different test forms reflects the same level of ability.

Research on the LSAT

Summaries of LSAT validity studies and other LSAT research can be found in member law school libraries and at LSAC.org.

To Inquire About Test Questions

If you find what you believe to be an error or ambiguity in a test question that affects your response to the question, contact LSAC by e-mail: LSATTS@LSAC.org, or write to Law School Admission Council, Test Development Group, PO Box 40, Newtown, PA 18940-0040.

HOW THIS PREPTEST DIFFERS FROM AN ACTUAL LSAT

This PrepTest is made up of the scored sections and writing sample from the actual disclosed LSAT administered in September 2018. However, it does not contain the extra, variable section that is used to pretest new test items of one of the three multiple-choice question types. The three multiple-choice question types may be in a different order in an actual LSAT than in this PrepTest. This is because the order of these question types is intentionally varied for each administration of the test.

THE THREE LSAT MULTIPLE-CHOICE QUESTION TYPES

The multiple-choice questions that make up most of the LSAT reflect a broad range of academic disciplines and are intended to give no advantage to candidates from a particular academic background.

The five sections of the test contain three different question types. The following material presents a general discussion of the nature of each question type and some strategies that can be used in answering them.

Analytical Reasoning Questions

Analytical Reasoning questions are designed to assess the ability to consider a group of facts and rules, and, given those facts and rules, determine what could or must be true. The specific scenarios associated with these questions are usually unrelated to law, since they are intended to be accessible to a wide range of test takers. However, the skills tested parallel those involved in determining what could or must be the case given a set of regulations, the terms of a contract, or the facts of a legal case in relation to the law. In Analytical Reasoning questions, you are asked to reason deductively from a set of statements and rules or principles that describe relationships among persons, things, or events.

Analytical Reasoning questions appear in sets, with each set based on a single passage. The passage used for each set of questions describes common ordering relationships or grouping relationships, or a combination of both types of relationships. Examples include scheduling employees for work shifts, assigning instructors to class sections, ordering tasks according to priority, and distributing grants for projects.

Analytical Reasoning questions test a range of deductive reasoning skills. These include:

- Comprehending the basic structure of a set of relationships by determining a complete solution to the problem posed (for example, an acceptable seating arrangement of all six diplomats around a table)

- Reasoning with conditional ("if-then") statements and recognizing logically equivalent formulations of such statements

- Inferring what could be true or must be true from given facts and rules

- Inferring what could be true or must be true from given facts and rules together with new information in the form of an additional or substitute fact or rule

- Recognizing when two statements are logically equivalent in context by identifying a condition or rule that could replace one of the original conditions while still resulting in the same possible outcomes

Analytical Reasoning questions reflect the kinds of detailed analyses of relationships and sets of constraints that a law student must perform in legal problem solving. For example, an Analytical Reasoning passage might describe six diplomats being seated around a table, following certain rules of protocol as to who can sit where. You, the test taker, must answer questions about the logical implications of given and new information. For example, you may be asked who can sit between diplomats X and Y, or who cannot sit next to X if W sits next to Y. Similarly, if you were a student in law school, you might be asked to analyze a scenario involving a set of particular circumstances and a set of governing rules in the form of constitutional provisions, statutes, administrative codes, or prior rulings that have been upheld. You might then be asked to determine the legal options in the scenario: what is required given the scenario, what is permissible given the scenario, and what is prohibited given the scenario. Or you might be asked to develop a "theory" for the case: when faced with an incomplete set of facts about the case, you must fill in the picture based on what is implied by the facts that are known. The problem could be elaborated by the addition of new information or hypotheticals.

No formal training in logic is required to answer these questions correctly. Analytical Reasoning questions are intended to be answered using knowledge, skills, and reasoning ability generally expected of college students and graduates.

Suggested Approach

Some people may prefer to answer first those questions about a passage that seem less difficult and then those that seem more difficult. In general, it is best to finish one passage before starting on another, because much time can be lost in returning to a passage and reestablishing familiarity with its relationships. However, if you are having great difficulty on one particular set of questions and are spending too much time on them, it may be to your advantage to skip that set of questions and go on to the next passage, returning to the problematic set of questions after you have finished the other questions in the section.

Do not assume that because the conditions for a set of questions look long or complicated, the questions based on those conditions will be especially difficult.

Read the passage carefully. Careful reading and analysis are necessary to determine the exact nature of the relationships involved in an Analytical Reasoning passage. Some relationships are fixed (for example, P and R must always work on the same project). Other relationships are variable (for example, Q must be assigned to either team 1 or team 3). Some relationships that are not stated explicitly in the conditions are implied by and can be deduced from those that are stated (for example, if one condition about paintings in a display specifies that Painting K must be to the left of Painting Y, and another specifies that Painting W must be to the left of Painting K, then it can be deduced that Painting W must be to the left of Painting Y).

In reading the conditions, do not introduce unwarranted assumptions. For instance, in a set of questions establishing relationships of height and weight among the members of a team, do not assume that a person who is taller than another person must weigh more than that person. As another example, suppose a set involves ordering and a question in the set asks what must be true if both X and Y must be earlier than Z; in this case, do not assume that X must be earlier than Y merely because X is mentioned before Y. All the information needed to answer each question is provided in the passage and the question itself.

The conditions are designed to be as clear as possible. Do not interpret the conditions as if they were intended to trick you. For example, if a question asks how many people could be eligible to serve on a committee, consider only those people named in the passage unless directed otherwise. When in doubt, read the conditions in their most obvious sense. Remember, however, that the language in the conditions is intended to be read for precise meaning. It is essential to pay particular attention to words that describe or limit relationships, such as "only," "exactly," "never," "always," "must be," "cannot be," and the like.

The result of this careful reading will be a clear picture of the structure of the relationships involved, including the kinds of relationships permitted, the participants in the relationships, and the range of possible actions or attributes for these participants.

Keep in mind question independence. Each question should be considered separately from the other questions in its set. No information, except what is given in the original conditions, should be carried over from one question to another.

In some cases a question will simply ask for conclusions to be drawn from the conditions as originally given. Some questions may, however, add information to the original conditions or temporarily suspend or replace one of the original conditions for the purpose of that question only. For example, if Question 1 adds the supposition "if P is sitting at table 2 …," this supposition should NOT be carried over to any other question in the set.

Consider highlighting text and using diagrams. Many people find it useful to underline key points in the passage and in each question. In addition, it may prove very helpful to draw a diagram to assist you in finding the solution to the problem.

In preparing for the test, you may wish to experiment with different types of diagrams. For a scheduling problem, a simple calendar-like diagram may be helpful. For a grouping problem, an array of labeled columns or rows may be useful.

Even though most people find diagrams to be very helpful, some people seldom use them, and for some individual questions no one will need a diagram. There is by no means universal agreement on which kind of diagram is best for which problem or in which cases a diagram is most useful. Do not be concerned if a particular problem in the test seems to be best approached without the use of a diagram.

Logical Reasoning Questions

Arguments are a fundamental part of the law, and analyzing arguments is a key element of legal analysis. Training in the law builds on a foundation of basic reasoning skills. Law students must draw on the skills of analyzing, evaluating, constructing, and refuting arguments. They need to be able to identify what information is relevant to an issue or argument and what impact further evidence might have. They need to be able to reconcile opposing positions and use arguments to persuade others.

Logical Reasoning questions evaluate the ability to analyze, critically evaluate, and complete arguments as they occur in ordinary language. The questions are based on short arguments drawn from a wide variety of sources, including newspapers, general interest magazines, scholarly publications, advertisements, and informal discourse. These arguments mirror legal reasoning in the types of arguments presented and in their complexity, though few of the arguments actually have law as a subject matter.

Each Logical Reasoning question requires you to read and comprehend a short passage, then answer one question (or, rarely, two questions) about it. The questions are designed to assess a wide range of skills involved in thinking critically, with an emphasis on skills that are central to legal reasoning.

These skills include:

- Recognizing the parts of an argument and their relationships

- Recognizing similarities and differences between patterns of reasoning

- Drawing well-supported conclusions

- Reasoning by analogy

- Recognizing misunderstandings or points of disagreement

- Determining how additional evidence affects an argument

- Detecting assumptions made by particular arguments

- Identifying and applying principles or rules

- Identifying flaws in arguments

- Identifying explanations

The questions do not presuppose specialized knowledge of logical terminology. For example, you will not be expected to know the meaning of specialized terms such as "ad hominem" or "syllogism." On the other hand, you will be expected to understand and critique the reasoning contained in arguments. This requires that you possess a university-level understanding of widely used concepts such as argument, premise, assumption, and conclusion.

Suggested Approach

Read each question carefully. Make sure that you understand the meaning of each part of the question. Make sure that you understand the meaning of each answer choice and the ways in which it may or may not relate to the question posed.

Do not pick a response simply because it is a true statement. Although true, it may not answer the question posed.

Answer each question on the basis of the information that is given, even if you do not agree with it. Work within the context provided by the passage. LSAT questions do not involve any tricks or hidden meanings.

Reading Comprehension Questions

Both law school and the practice of law revolve around extensive reading of highly varied, dense, argumentative, and expository texts (for example, cases, codes, contracts, briefs, decisions, evidence). This reading must be exacting, distinguishing precisely what is said from what is not said. It involves comparison, analysis, synthesis, and application (for example, of principles and rules). It involves drawing appropriate inferences and applying ideas and arguments to new contexts. Law school reading also requires the ability to grasp unfamiliar subject matter and the ability to penetrate difficult and challenging material.

The purpose of LSAT Reading Comprehension questions is to measure the ability to read, with understanding and insight, examples of lengthy and complex materials similar to those commonly encountered in law school. The Reading Comprehension section of the LSAT contains four sets of reading questions, each set consisting of a selection of reading material followed by five to eight questions. The reading selection in three of the four sets consists of a single reading passage; the other set contains two related shorter passages. Sets with two passages are a variant of Reading Comprehension called Comparative Reading, which was introduced in June 2007.

Comparative Reading questions concern the relationships between the two passages, such as those of generalization/instance, principle/application, or point/counterpoint. Law school work often requires reading two or more texts in conjunction with each other and understanding their relationships. For example, a law student may read a trial court decision together with an appellate court decision that overturns it, or identify the fact pattern from a hypothetical suit together with the potentially controlling case law.

Reading selections for LSAT Reading Comprehension questions are drawn from a wide range of subjects in the humanities, the social sciences, the biological and physical sciences, and areas related to the law. Generally, the selections are densely written, use high-level vocabulary, and contain sophisticated argument or complex rhetorical structure (for example, multiple points of view). Reading Comprehension questions require you to read carefully and accurately, to determine the relationships among the various parts of the reading selection, and to draw reasonable inferences from the material in the selection. The questions may ask about the following characteristics of a passage or pair of passages:

- The main idea or primary purpose

- Information that is explicitly stated

- Information or ideas that can be inferred

- The meaning or purpose of words or phrases as used in context

- The organization or structure

- The application of information in the selection to a new context

- Principles that function in the selection

- Analogies to claims or arguments in the selection

- An author's attitude as revealed in the tone of a passage or the language used

- The impact of new information on claims or arguments in the selection

Suggested Approach

Since reading selections are drawn from many different disciplines and sources, you should not be discouraged if you encounter material with which you are not familiar. It is important to remember that questions are to be answered exclusively on the basis of the information provided in the selection. There is no particular knowledge that you are expected to bring to the test, and you should not make inferences based on any prior knowledge of a subject that you may have. You may, however, wish to defer working on a set of questions that seems particularly difficult or unfamiliar until after you have dealt with sets you find easier.

Strategies. One question that often arises in connection with Reading Comprehension has to do with the most effective and efficient order in which to read the selections and questions. Possible approaches include:

- reading the selection very closely and then answering the questions;

- reading the questions first, reading the selection closely, and then returning to the questions; or

- skimming the selection and questions very quickly, then rereading the selection closely and answering the questions.

Test takers are different, and the best strategy for one might not be the best strategy for another. In preparing for the test, therefore, you might want to experiment with the different strategies and decide what works most effectively for you.

Remember that your strategy must be effective under timed conditions. For this reason, the first strategy—reading the selection very closely and then answering the questions—may be the most effective for you. Nonetheless, if you believe that one of the other strategies

might be more effective for you, you should try it out and assess your performance using it.

Reading the selection. Whatever strategy you choose, you should give the passage or pair of passages at least one careful reading before answering the questions. Try to distinguish main ideas from supporting ideas, and opinions or attitudes from factual, objective information. Note transitions from one idea to the next and identify the relationships among the different ideas or parts of a passage, or between the two passages in Comparative Reading sets. Consider how and why an author makes points and draws conclusions. Be sensitive to implications of what the passages say.

You may find it helpful to mark key parts of passages. For example, you might underline main ideas or important arguments, and you might circle transitional words—"although," "nevertheless," "correspondingly," and the like—that will help you map the structure of a passage. Also, you might note descriptive words that will help you identify an author's attitude toward a particular idea or person.

Answering the Questions

- Always read all the answer choices before selecting the best answer. The best answer choice is the one that most accurately and completely answers the question being posed.

- Respond to the specific question being asked. Do not pick an answer choice simply because it is a true statement. For example, picking a true statement might yield an incorrect answer to a question in which you are asked to identify an author's position on an issue, since you are not being asked to evaluate the truth of the author's position but only to correctly identify what that position is.

- Answer the questions only on the basis of the information provided in the selection. Your own views, interpretations, or opinions, and those you have heard from others, may sometimes conflict with those expressed in a reading selection; however, you are expected to work within the context provided by the reading selection. You should not expect to agree with everything you encounter in Reading Comprehension passages.

THE WRITING SAMPLE

On the day of the test, you will be asked to write one sample essay. LSAC does not score the writing sample, but copies are sent to all law schools to which you apply. According to a 2015 LSAC survey of 129 United States and Canadian law schools, almost all utilize the writing sample in evaluating some applications for admission. Failure to respond to writing sample prompts and frivolous responses have been used by law schools as grounds for rejection of applications for admission.

In developing and implementing the writing sample portion of the LSAT, LSAC has operated on the following premises: First, law schools and the legal profession value highly the ability to communicate effectively in writing. Second, it is important to encourage potential law students to develop effective writing skills. Third, a sample of an applicant's writing, produced under controlled conditions, is a potentially useful indication of that person's writing ability. Fourth, the writing sample can serve as an independent check on other writing submitted by applicants as part of the admission process. Finally, writing samples may be useful for diagnostic purposes related to improving a candidate's writing.

The writing prompt presents a decision problem. You are asked to make a choice between two positions or courses of action. Both of the choices are defensible, and you are given criteria and facts on which to base your decision. There is no "right" or "wrong" position to take on the topic, so the quality of each test taker's response is a function not of which choice is made, but of how well or poorly the choice is supported and how well or poorly the other choice is criticized.

The LSAT writing prompt was designed and validated by legal education professionals. Since it involves writing based on fact sets and criteria, the writing sample gives applicants the opportunity to demonstrate the type of argumentative writing that is required in law school, although the topics are usually nonlegal.

You will have 35 minutes in which to plan and write an essay on the topic you receive. Read the topic and the accompanying directions carefully. You will probably find it best to spend a few minutes considering the topic and organizing your thoughts before you begin writing. In your essay, be sure to develop your ideas fully, leaving time, if possible, to review what you have written. Do not write on a topic other than the one specified. Writing on a topic of your own choice is not acceptable.

No special knowledge is required or expected for this writing exercise. Law schools are interested in the reasoning, clarity, organization, language usage, and writing mechanics displayed in your essay. How well you write is more important than how much you write. Confine your essay to the blocked, lined area on the front and back of the separate Writing Sample Response Sheet. Only that area will be reproduced for law schools. Be sure that your writing is legible.

TAKING THE PREPTEST UNDER SIMULATED LSAT CONDITIONS

One important way to prepare for the LSAT is to simulate the day of the test by taking a practice test under actual time constraints. Taking a practice test under timed conditions helps you to estimate the amount of time you can afford to spend on each question in a section and to determine the question types on which you may need additional practice.

Since the LSAT is a timed test, it is important to use your allotted time wisely. During the test, you may work only on the section designated by the test supervisor. You cannot devote extra time to a difficult section and make up that time on a section you find easier. In pacing yourself, and checking your answers, you should think of each section of the test as a separate minitest.

Be sure that you answer every question on the test. When you do not know the correct answer to a question, first eliminate the responses that you know are incorrect, then make your best guess among the remaining choices. Do not be afraid to guess as there is no penalty for incorrect answers.

When you take a practice test, abide by all the requirements specified in the directions and keep strictly within the specified time limits. Work without a rest period. When you take an actual test, you will have only a short break—usually 10–15 minutes—after SECTION III.

When taken under conditions as much like actual testing conditions as possible, a practice test provides very useful preparation for taking the LSAT.

Official directions for the four multiple-choice sections and the writing sample are included in this PrepTest so that you can approximate actual testing conditions as you practice.

To take the test:

- Set a timer for 35 minutes. Answer all the questions in SECTION I of this PrepTest. Stop working on that section when the 35 minutes have elapsed.

- Repeat, allowing yourself 35 minutes each for sections II, III, and IV.

- Set the timer again for 35 minutes, then prepare your response to the writing sample topic at the end of this PrepTest.

- Refer to "Computing Your Score" for the PrepTest for instruction on evaluating your performance. An answer key is provided for that purpose.

The practice test that follows consists of four sections corresponding to the four scored sections of the September 2018 LSAT. Also reprinted is the September 2018 unscored writing sample topic.

General Directions for the LSAT Answer Sheet

This portion of the test consists of five multiple-choice sections, each with a time limit of 35 minutes. The supervisor will tell you when to begin and end each section. If you finish a section before time is called, you may check your work on that section **only**; do not turn to any other section of the test book and do not work on any other section either in the test book or on the answer sheet.

There are several different types of questions on the test, and each question type has its own directions. **Be sure you understand the directions for each question type before attempting to answer any questions in that section.**

Not everyone will finish all the questions in the time allowed. Do not hurry, but work steadily and as quickly as you can without sacrificing accuracy. You are advised to use your time effectively. If a question seems too difficult, go on to the next one and return to the difficult question after completing the section. **MARK THE BEST ANSWER YOU CAN FOR EVERY QUESTION. NO DEDUCTIONS WILL BE MADE FOR WRONG ANSWERS. YOUR SCORE WILL BE BASED ONLY ON THE NUMBER OF QUESTIONS YOU ANSWER CORRECTLY.**

ALL YOUR ANSWERS MUST BE MARKED ON THE ANSWER SHEET. Answer spaces for each question are lettered to correspond with the letters of the potential answers to each question in the test book. After you have decided which of the answers is correct, blacken the corresponding space on the answer sheet. **BE SURE THAT EACH MARK IS BLACK AND COMPLETELY FILLS THE ANSWER SPACE.** Give only one answer to each question. If you change an answer, be sure that all previous marks are **erased completely.** Since the answer sheet is machine scored, incomplete erasures may be interpreted as intended answers. **ANSWERS RECORDED IN THE TEST BOOK WILL NOT BE SCORED.**

There may be more question numbers on this answer sheet than there are questions in a section. Do not be concerned, but be certain that the section and number of the question you are answering matches the answer sheet section and question number. Additional answer spaces in any answer sheet section should be left blank. Begin your next section in the number one answer space for that section.

LSAC takes various steps to ensure that answer sheets are returned from test centers in a timely manner for processing. In the unlikely event that an answer sheet is not received, LSAC will permit the examinee either to retest at no additional fee or to receive a refund of his or her LSAT fee. **THESE REMEDIES ARE THE ONLY REMEDIES AVAILABLE IN THE UNLIKELY EVENT THAT AN ANSWER SHEET IS NOT RECEIVED BY LSAC.**

HOW DID YOU PREPARE FOR THE LSAT?
(Select all that apply.)

Responses to this item are voluntary and will be used for statistical research purposes only.

- ○ By using Khan Academy's official LSAT practice material.
- ○ By taking the free sample questions and/or free sample LSAT available on LSAC's website.
- ○ By working through official LSAT *PrepTest* and/or other LSAC test prep products.
- ○ By using LSAT prep books or software **not** published by LSAC.
- ○ By attending a commercial test preparation or coaching course.
- ○ By attending a test preparation or coaching course offered through an undergraduate institution.
- ○ Self study.
- ○ Other preparation.
- ○ No preparation.

CERTIFYING STATEMENT

Please write the following statement. Sign and date.

I certify that I am the examinee whose name appears on this answer sheet and that I am here to take the LSAT for the sole purpose of being considered for admission to law school. I further certify that I will neither assist nor receive assistance from any other candidate, and I agree not to copy, retain, or transmit examination questions in any form or discuss them with any other person.

SIGNATURE: _____

TODAY'S DATE: _____/_____/_____
MONTH DAY YEAR

DO NOT WRITE IN THIS BOX.

FOR LSAC USE ONLY

Law School Admission Council

A

·INSTRUCTIONS FOR COMPLETING THE BIOGRAPHICAL AREA ARE ON THE BACK COVER OF YOUR TEST BOOKLET.
USE ONLY A NO. 2 OR HB PENCIL TO COMPLETE THIS ANSWER SHEET. DO NOT USE INK.

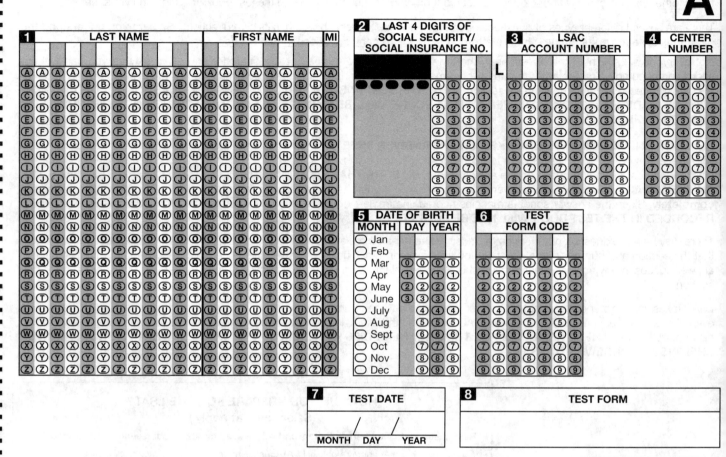

1 LAST NAME · FIRST NAME · MI

2 LAST 4 DIGITS OF SOCIAL SECURITY/ SOCIAL INSURANCE NO. L

3 LSAC ACCOUNT NUMBER

4 CENTER NUMBER

5 DATE OF BIRTH
MONTH · DAY · YEAR
○ Jan ○ Feb ○ Mar ○ Apr ○ May ○ June ○ July ○ Aug ○ Sept ○ Oct ○ Nov ○ Dec

6 TEST FORM CODE

7 TEST DATE
MONTH / DAY / YEAR

8 TEST FORM

Law School Admission Test

Mark one and only one answer to each question. Be sure to fill in completely the space for your intended answer choice. If you erase, do so completely. Make no stray marks.

9 TEST BOOK SERIAL NO.

SECTION 1	SECTION 2	SECTION 3	SECTION 4	SECTION 5
1 Ⓐ Ⓑ Ⓒ Ⓓ Ⓔ	1 Ⓐ Ⓑ Ⓒ Ⓓ Ⓔ	1 Ⓐ Ⓑ Ⓒ Ⓓ Ⓔ	1 Ⓐ Ⓑ Ⓒ Ⓓ Ⓔ	1 Ⓐ Ⓑ Ⓒ Ⓓ Ⓔ
2 Ⓐ Ⓑ Ⓒ Ⓓ Ⓔ	2 Ⓐ Ⓑ Ⓒ Ⓓ Ⓔ	2 Ⓐ Ⓑ Ⓒ Ⓓ Ⓔ	2 Ⓐ Ⓑ Ⓒ Ⓓ Ⓔ	2 Ⓐ Ⓑ Ⓒ Ⓓ Ⓔ
3 Ⓐ Ⓑ Ⓒ Ⓓ Ⓔ	3 Ⓐ Ⓑ Ⓒ Ⓓ Ⓔ	3 Ⓐ Ⓑ Ⓒ Ⓓ Ⓔ	3 Ⓐ Ⓑ Ⓒ Ⓓ Ⓔ	3 Ⓐ Ⓑ Ⓒ Ⓓ Ⓔ
4 Ⓐ Ⓑ Ⓒ Ⓓ Ⓔ	4 Ⓐ Ⓑ Ⓒ Ⓓ Ⓔ	4 Ⓐ Ⓑ Ⓒ Ⓓ Ⓔ	4 Ⓐ Ⓑ Ⓒ Ⓓ Ⓔ	4 Ⓐ Ⓑ Ⓒ Ⓓ Ⓔ
5 Ⓐ Ⓑ Ⓒ Ⓓ Ⓔ	5 Ⓐ Ⓑ Ⓒ Ⓓ Ⓔ	5 Ⓐ Ⓑ Ⓒ Ⓓ Ⓔ	5 Ⓐ Ⓑ Ⓒ Ⓓ Ⓔ	5 Ⓐ Ⓑ Ⓒ Ⓓ Ⓔ
6 Ⓐ Ⓑ Ⓒ Ⓓ Ⓔ	6 Ⓐ Ⓑ Ⓒ Ⓓ Ⓔ	6 Ⓐ Ⓑ Ⓒ Ⓓ Ⓔ	6 Ⓐ Ⓑ Ⓒ Ⓓ Ⓔ	6 Ⓐ Ⓑ Ⓒ Ⓓ Ⓔ
7 Ⓐ Ⓑ Ⓒ Ⓓ Ⓔ	7 Ⓐ Ⓑ Ⓒ Ⓓ Ⓔ	7 Ⓐ Ⓑ Ⓒ Ⓓ Ⓔ	7 Ⓐ Ⓑ Ⓒ Ⓓ Ⓔ	7 Ⓐ Ⓑ Ⓒ Ⓓ Ⓔ
8 Ⓐ Ⓑ Ⓒ Ⓓ Ⓔ	8 Ⓐ Ⓑ Ⓒ Ⓓ Ⓔ	8 Ⓐ Ⓑ Ⓒ Ⓓ Ⓔ	8 Ⓐ Ⓑ Ⓒ Ⓓ Ⓔ	8 Ⓐ Ⓑ Ⓒ Ⓓ Ⓔ
9 Ⓐ Ⓑ Ⓒ Ⓓ Ⓔ	9 Ⓐ Ⓑ Ⓒ Ⓓ Ⓔ	9 Ⓐ Ⓑ Ⓒ Ⓓ Ⓔ	9 Ⓐ Ⓑ Ⓒ Ⓓ Ⓔ	9 Ⓐ Ⓑ Ⓒ Ⓓ Ⓔ
10 Ⓐ Ⓑ Ⓒ Ⓓ Ⓔ	10 Ⓐ Ⓑ Ⓒ Ⓓ Ⓔ	10 Ⓐ Ⓑ Ⓒ Ⓓ Ⓔ	10 Ⓐ Ⓑ Ⓒ Ⓓ Ⓔ	10 Ⓐ Ⓑ Ⓒ Ⓓ Ⓔ
11 Ⓐ Ⓑ Ⓒ Ⓓ Ⓔ	11 Ⓐ Ⓑ Ⓒ Ⓓ Ⓔ	11 Ⓐ Ⓑ Ⓒ Ⓓ Ⓔ	11 Ⓐ Ⓑ Ⓒ Ⓓ Ⓔ	11 Ⓐ Ⓑ Ⓒ Ⓓ Ⓔ
12 Ⓐ Ⓑ Ⓒ Ⓓ Ⓔ	12 Ⓐ Ⓑ Ⓒ Ⓓ Ⓔ	12 Ⓐ Ⓑ Ⓒ Ⓓ Ⓔ	12 Ⓐ Ⓑ Ⓒ Ⓓ Ⓔ	12 Ⓐ Ⓑ Ⓒ Ⓓ Ⓔ
13 Ⓐ Ⓑ Ⓒ Ⓓ Ⓔ	13 Ⓐ Ⓑ Ⓒ Ⓓ Ⓔ	13 Ⓐ Ⓑ Ⓒ Ⓓ Ⓔ	13 Ⓐ Ⓑ Ⓒ Ⓓ Ⓔ	13 Ⓐ Ⓑ Ⓒ Ⓓ Ⓔ
14 Ⓐ Ⓑ Ⓒ Ⓓ Ⓔ	14 Ⓐ Ⓑ Ⓒ Ⓓ Ⓔ	14 Ⓐ Ⓑ Ⓒ Ⓓ Ⓔ	14 Ⓐ Ⓑ Ⓒ Ⓓ Ⓔ	14 Ⓐ Ⓑ Ⓒ Ⓓ Ⓔ
15 Ⓐ Ⓑ Ⓒ Ⓓ Ⓔ	15 Ⓐ Ⓑ Ⓒ Ⓓ Ⓔ	15 Ⓐ Ⓑ Ⓒ Ⓓ Ⓔ	15 Ⓐ Ⓑ Ⓒ Ⓓ Ⓔ	15 Ⓐ Ⓑ Ⓒ Ⓓ Ⓔ
16 Ⓐ Ⓑ Ⓒ Ⓓ Ⓔ	16 Ⓐ Ⓑ Ⓒ Ⓓ Ⓔ	16 Ⓐ Ⓑ Ⓒ Ⓓ Ⓔ	16 Ⓐ Ⓑ Ⓒ Ⓓ Ⓔ	16 Ⓐ Ⓑ Ⓒ Ⓓ Ⓔ
17 Ⓐ Ⓑ Ⓒ Ⓓ Ⓔ	17 Ⓐ Ⓑ Ⓒ Ⓓ Ⓔ	17 Ⓐ Ⓑ Ⓒ Ⓓ Ⓔ	17 Ⓐ Ⓑ Ⓒ Ⓓ Ⓔ	17 Ⓐ Ⓑ Ⓒ Ⓓ Ⓔ
18 Ⓐ Ⓑ Ⓒ Ⓓ Ⓔ	18 Ⓐ Ⓑ Ⓒ Ⓓ Ⓔ	18 Ⓐ Ⓑ Ⓒ Ⓓ Ⓔ	18 Ⓐ Ⓑ Ⓒ Ⓓ Ⓔ	18 Ⓐ Ⓑ Ⓒ Ⓓ Ⓔ
19 Ⓐ Ⓑ Ⓒ Ⓓ Ⓔ	19 Ⓐ Ⓑ Ⓒ Ⓓ Ⓔ	19 Ⓐ Ⓑ Ⓒ Ⓓ Ⓔ	19 Ⓐ Ⓑ Ⓒ Ⓓ Ⓔ	19 Ⓐ Ⓑ Ⓒ Ⓓ Ⓔ
20 Ⓐ Ⓑ Ⓒ Ⓓ Ⓔ	20 Ⓐ Ⓑ Ⓒ Ⓓ Ⓔ	20 Ⓐ Ⓑ Ⓒ Ⓓ Ⓔ	20 Ⓐ Ⓑ Ⓒ Ⓓ Ⓔ	20 Ⓐ Ⓑ Ⓒ Ⓓ Ⓔ
21 Ⓐ Ⓑ Ⓒ Ⓓ Ⓔ	21 Ⓐ Ⓑ Ⓒ Ⓓ Ⓔ	21 Ⓐ Ⓑ Ⓒ Ⓓ Ⓔ	21 Ⓐ Ⓑ Ⓒ Ⓓ Ⓔ	21 Ⓐ Ⓑ Ⓒ Ⓓ Ⓔ
22 Ⓐ Ⓑ Ⓒ Ⓓ Ⓔ	22 Ⓐ Ⓑ Ⓒ Ⓓ Ⓔ	22 Ⓐ Ⓑ Ⓒ Ⓓ Ⓔ	22 Ⓐ Ⓑ Ⓒ Ⓓ Ⓔ	22 Ⓐ Ⓑ Ⓒ Ⓓ Ⓔ
23 Ⓐ Ⓑ Ⓒ Ⓓ Ⓔ	23 Ⓐ Ⓑ Ⓒ Ⓓ Ⓔ	23 Ⓐ Ⓑ Ⓒ Ⓓ Ⓔ	23 Ⓐ Ⓑ Ⓒ Ⓓ Ⓔ	23 Ⓐ Ⓑ Ⓒ Ⓓ Ⓔ
24 Ⓐ Ⓑ Ⓒ Ⓓ Ⓔ	24 Ⓐ Ⓑ Ⓒ Ⓓ Ⓔ	24 Ⓐ Ⓑ Ⓒ Ⓓ Ⓔ	24 Ⓐ Ⓑ Ⓒ Ⓓ Ⓔ	24 Ⓐ Ⓑ Ⓒ Ⓓ Ⓔ
25 Ⓐ Ⓑ Ⓒ Ⓓ Ⓔ	25 Ⓐ Ⓑ Ⓒ Ⓓ Ⓔ	25 Ⓐ Ⓑ Ⓒ Ⓓ Ⓔ	25 Ⓐ Ⓑ Ⓒ Ⓓ Ⓔ	25 Ⓐ Ⓑ Ⓒ Ⓓ Ⓔ
26 Ⓐ Ⓑ Ⓒ Ⓓ Ⓔ	26 Ⓐ Ⓑ Ⓒ Ⓓ Ⓔ	26 Ⓐ Ⓑ Ⓒ Ⓓ Ⓔ	26 Ⓐ Ⓑ Ⓒ Ⓓ Ⓔ	26 Ⓐ Ⓑ Ⓒ Ⓓ Ⓔ
27 Ⓐ Ⓑ Ⓒ Ⓓ Ⓔ	27 Ⓐ Ⓑ Ⓒ Ⓓ Ⓔ	27 Ⓐ Ⓑ Ⓒ Ⓓ Ⓔ	27 Ⓐ Ⓑ Ⓒ Ⓓ Ⓔ	27 Ⓐ Ⓑ Ⓒ Ⓓ Ⓔ
28 Ⓐ Ⓑ Ⓒ Ⓓ Ⓔ	28 Ⓐ Ⓑ Ⓒ Ⓓ Ⓔ	28 Ⓐ Ⓑ Ⓒ Ⓓ Ⓔ	28 Ⓐ Ⓑ Ⓒ Ⓓ Ⓔ	28 Ⓐ Ⓑ Ⓒ Ⓓ Ⓔ
29 Ⓐ Ⓑ Ⓒ Ⓓ Ⓔ	29 Ⓐ Ⓑ Ⓒ Ⓓ Ⓔ	29 Ⓐ Ⓑ Ⓒ Ⓓ Ⓔ	29 Ⓐ Ⓑ Ⓒ Ⓓ Ⓔ	29 Ⓐ Ⓑ Ⓒ Ⓓ Ⓔ
30 Ⓐ Ⓑ Ⓒ Ⓓ Ⓔ	30 Ⓐ Ⓑ Ⓒ Ⓓ Ⓔ	30 Ⓐ Ⓑ Ⓒ Ⓓ Ⓔ	30 Ⓐ Ⓑ Ⓒ Ⓓ Ⓔ	30 Ⓐ Ⓑ Ⓒ Ⓓ Ⓔ

10 PLEASE PRINT INFORMATION

LAST NAME

FIRST NAME

DATE OF BIRTH

● Ⓑ

Law School Admission Council

THE PREPTEST

SECTION I

Time—35 minutes

27 Questions

Directions: Each set of questions in this section is based on a single passage or a pair of passages. The questions are to be answered on the basis of what is <u>stated</u> or <u>implied</u> in the passage or pair of passages. For some questions, more than one of the choices could conceivably answer the question. However, you are to choose the <u>best</u> answer; that is, choose the response that most accurately and completely answers the question and mark that response on your answer sheet.

The United States Supreme Court's 1948 ruling in *Shelley v. Kraemer* famously disallowed state courts from enforcing racially restrictive covenants. Such covenants are, in essence, private legal obligations
(5) included in the deed to a property requiring that only members of a certain race be allowed to occupy the property. Because it prohibited the enforcement of these covenants, the Court's decision in *Shelley v. Kraemer* is justly celebrated for overturning a key
(10) instrument of housing discrimination. However, while few would deny that racially restrictive covenants are unjust, the stated legal rationale for the *Shelley* decision has nevertheless proven to be problematic.

The *Shelley* Court relied on the Fourteenth
(15) Amendment to the U.S. Constitution, which grants equal protection under the law to all U.S. citizens. This amendment had long been held to apply to state actors but not individuals. *Shelley* did not purport to alter this. But where, then, was the state action that is
(20) necessary for invoking the Fourteenth Amendment, given that the restrictive covenants were private contracts? The Court's answer was that although the restrictive covenants themselves were perfectly legal, judicial enforcement of the covenants violated the
(25) Fourteenth Amendment because responsibility for a contract's substantive provisions should be attributed to the state when a court enforces it. According to this "attribution" rationale, courts could enforce only those contractual provisions that could have been enacted
(30) into general law. Because the Fourteenth Amendment would not have allowed a law that banned members of a certain race from purchasing property, it followed from *Shelley*'s analysis that judicial enforcement of racially restrictive covenants also was unconstitutional.

(35) *Shelley*'s attribution logic threatened to dissolve the distinction between state action, to which Fourteenth Amendment limitations apply, and private action, which falls outside of the Fourteenth Amendment's purview. After all, *Shelley*'s approach,
(40) consistently applied, would require individuals to conform their private agreements to constitutional standards whenever, as is almost always the case, the individuals want the option of later seeking judicial enforcement. Primarily for this reason, neither the
(45) Supreme Court nor lower courts later applied *Shelley*'s approach. Courts routinely enforce contracts whose substantive provisions could not have been constitutionally enacted by government. For instance, courts regularly enforce settlement agreements that
(50) limit the settling party's ability to speak publicly in various respects, despite the fact that statutory

limitations on the identical speech would represent an unconstitutional violation of free speech.

Additionally, there is a particularly noxious aspect
(55) of the *Shelley* Court's analytics—namely, the Court's conclusion that racially restrictive covenants themselves were perfectly legal. The legal rationale behind the *Shelley* decision thus failed to target the genuine problem with racially restrictive covenants:
(60) what was troubling was not the covenants' enforcement but their substantive content.

1. The primary purpose of the passage is to

(A) question the reasoning behind a particular judicial decision
(B) draw a distinction between private action and state action
(C) defend the way in which scholars and courts have traditionally explained a particular judicial decision
(D) highlight the shortcomings of the U.S. Constitution
(E) extend the rationale offered in a particular judicial decision to additional cases

2. An answer to which one of the following questions would be most relevant to determining whether an action can be classified a "state action" (line 19), as the author uses that phrase in the second paragraph?

(A) What range of people can the action be expected to affect?
(B) To what agent can performance of the action be ascribed?
(C) What principle or principles can be said to govern the action?
(D) In what ways can the action be expected to affect others?
(E) What motivations can be attributed to those performing the action?

GO ON TO THE NEXT PAGE.

3. The author's attitude towards the reasoning offered in the U.S. Supreme Court's decision in *Shelley v. Kraemer* is most accurately reflected in the author's use of which one of the following phrases?

   (A) "famously disallowed" (line 2)
   (B) "justly celebrated" (line 9)
   (C) "perfectly legal" (line 23)
   (D) "consistently applied" (line 40)
   (E) "noxious aspect" (line 54)

4. Which one of the following describes an attribution of responsibility that is most analogous to the attribution central to what the author refers to as *Shelley*'s "attribution" rationale (line 28)?

   (A) If a trucking company fails to properly inspect its vehicles, the company can be held responsible for any accidents in which those vehicles are involved.
   (B) If an individual signs a private contract, that person can be held responsible for the provisions of that contract even if the person did not read or comprehend those provisions.
   (C) If a newspaper publishes a columnist's op-ed piece, the newspaper, and not just the columnist, can be held responsible for the content of the piece.
   (D) If a person is in a position to rescue someone in peril, but chooses not to do so, that person can be held responsible for any injuries suffered by the person in peril.
   (E) If a company discovers that it has manufactured and distributed a faulty product, the company is responsible for issuing a recall of that product.

5. In the second paragraph, the author asks the question, "…where, then, was the state action that is necessary for invoking the Fourteenth Amendment, given that the restrictive covenants were private contracts?" (lines 19–22) primarily in order to

   (A) demonstrate the conceptual incoherence of a distinction employed by the *Shelley* Court
   (B) highlight a potentially confusing issue central to understanding the *Shelley* Court's decision
   (C) suggest that the *Shelley* Court did not properly attend to the facts of the case in its decision
   (D) cast suspicion on the motivations of the individual judges who served on the *Shelley* Court
   (E) challenge the presuppositions upon which the Fourteenth Amendment to the U.S. Constitution is based

6. Which one of the following principles is most clearly operative in the author's argument?

   (A) If a judicial decision is deemed by legal scholars to be problematic, subsequent courts should refrain from appealing to that decision.
   (B) If a private agreement is deemed judicially unenforceable, the substantive content of that agreement should be considered for inclusion in a statute.
   (C) If a judicial decision fails to address the most troubling aspect of a practice, then measures should be taken to prevent this practice from continuing in an altered form.
   (D) If courts are hesitant to apply the rationale given in a past decision, this should be taken as evidence that the rationale is questionable.
   (E) If the rationale given in a judicial decision is found to be controversial, the decision should be supported by offering a new rationale.

GO ON TO THE NEXT PAGE.

Through years of excavations and careful analysis
of her finds around Krasnyi Yar in Kazakhstan,
archaeologist Sandra Olsen has assembled what may
be evidence of the earliest known people to have
(5) domesticated and ridden horses, a momentous
development in human history. In remains of pit
houses of the Botai people, who inhabited this area
some 6,000 years ago, are large numbers of bones,
90 percent of them from horses. It is not immediately
(10) evident whether the horses were wild or domesticated,
because unlike other animals such as dogs and sheep,
domestic horses' bones are not morphologically
different from those of their wild counterparts. So
Olsen relies heavily on statistical tabulations of the
(15) Botai horses by sex and age at death, looking for
mortality patterns that might correlate with
expectations regarding domesticated herds or wild
victims of hunting.

Herders of domesticated animals used for meat or
(20) milk typically kill off all but a few males before they
are fully mature, but not the females, and archaeologists
have evidence of a similar pattern for prehistoric goat
herding. At the Botai sites, however, Olsen has found
that most of the male horses were fully grown and
(25) slightly outnumber the females. One might suppose,
then, that they were wild rather than domesticated
animals; with many large animal species, hunters
would preferentially target adult males so as to
maximize size and meat yield. However, it is different
(30) with horses. Wild horses live in two types of groups:
families consisting of one stallion, six or so adult
females, and their young; and bachelor pods consisting
of a few males. The families stick together when
attacked, but the male groups tend to scatter, so to
(35) maximize success in hunting horses, one would target
the families. Thus, if the Botai had merely hunted
horses, Olsen argues, the proportion of adult male
bones should be lower. But if they were in domesticated
herds, why were the young males not culled, as would
(40) typically occur with, say, herds of goats? Olsen reasons
that if the Botai had indeed begun riding, they would
likely have kept males alive to ride.

Another clue that at least some of the horses may
have been domesticated and that some may have even
(45) been ridden is in the fact that their remains include full
skeletons, entire vertebral columns, and pelvises. It is
unreasonable to suppose that hunters dragged whole
1,000-pound carcasses back to their dwellings. Olsen
reasons that these were probably domesticated horses,
(50) together with, perhaps, some wild ones hunted and
transported using the power of domesticated horses.
A number of these nearly whole horse skeletons were
discovered buried in a carefully arranged pattern with
some of the only human remains yet found in the area,
(55) which further suggests a relationship to horses beyond
that of merely hunting them as a source of meat.

7. Which one of the following most accurately expresses
the main point of the passage?

(A) Olsen's careful analysis of her finds in
Kazakhstan illustrates the kinds of conclusions
that archaeologists can draw based on a
correlation between statistical information
and expectations.
(B) Olsen's excavations and analysis of her finds in
Kazakhstan indicate that horses played a critical
role in Botai culture.
(C) Olsen's findings regarding bones excavated
from ancient Botai dwellings provide evidence
that the Botai people domesticated horses and
may have ridden them.
(D) Olsen's findings regarding excavations from
ancient Botai dwellings provide evidence
confirming that the domestication of horses was
a momentous development in human history.
(E) Olsen's findings regarding the excavation of
horse skeletons and human remains from Botai
dwellings suggest that horses were revered by
the Botai people.

8. Which one of the following most accurately describes
the author's attitude toward the conclusions that
Olsen reaches?

(A) forthright advocacy
(B) implicit endorsement
(C) critical ambivalence
(D) reasoned skepticism
(E) general disagreement

9. Which one of the following could replace the word
"beyond" in line 55 while least altering the meaning of
the sentence in which it appears?

(A) basically parallel to
(B) more elusive than
(C) hard to grasp in relation to
(D) less clearly defined than
(E) more complex than

GO ON TO THE NEXT PAGE.

10. If the horse remains found at the Botai sites had consisted primarily of the bones of fully grown females and young males, the findings would have provided evidence for which one of the following hypotheses?

(A) The Botai targeted male pods when hunting horses.

(B) The Botai caught, trained, and rode only wild horses.

(C) The Botai had domesticated horses but did not ride them.

(D) The Botai had developed sources of food other than horses.

(E) The Botai incorporated the remains of horses into their cultural rituals.

11. Based on the discussion in the passage, the author would be most likely to agree with which one of the following statements?

(A) Developing mortality patterns based on an examination of excavated animal remains is always required in order to establish whether a prehistoric culture domesticated animals.

(B) An analysis of evidence at a particular archaeological site is not necessarily conclusive unless it is corroborated by evidence at similar archaeological sites from the same era.

(C) Any prehistoric culture that consciously arranges the bones of animals in complex patterns should be considered to have reached a high level of social organization.

(D) The interpretation of archaeological finds at prehistoric sites often requires a consideration of facts beyond those that can be determined from the excavated remains alone.

(E) The morphological differences between wild and domesticated prehistoric animals help to explain why some modern animals are more easily domesticated than others.

12. The reference by the author of the passage to the practices of herders of domesticated animals (lines 19–21) serves primarily as

(A) a point of comparison for reaching conclusions about the use of horses by the Botai

(B) an example of an earlier case that, like the Botai case, is inconsistent with accepted hypotheses concerning the domestication of horses

(C) a refutation of traditional beliefs and assumptions about Botai goat herding

(D) a simplification of a hypothesis about the relationship between humans and animals in cultures 6,000 years ago

(E) an analogy meant to clarify the facts known about the domestication of animals by the Botai 6,000 years ago

13. Which one of the following most accurately describes the organization of the passage?

(A) A set of findings is described and then various explanations of the findings are evaluated.

(B) A set of specific observations is enumerated and then a general conclusion is drawn from those observations.

(C) A general principle is presented and then examples of the application of the principle are given.

(D) A hypothesis is outlined and then a line of reasoning in support of that hypothesis is developed.

(E) A proposition is stated and then arguments both for and against the proposition are summarized.

14. Data from which one of the following sources would be most relevant to evaluating Olsen's hypothesis?

(A) tabulation of the number of butchered horse bones versus untouched horse bones in a Botai archaeological site

(B) tabulation of the number of sheep and goat bones versus the number of horse bones in a Botai archaeological site

(C) determination of the number of hunting tribes contemporary with the Botai as opposed to the number of modern hunting tribes in the same area

(D) analysis of mortality patterns in the remains of any other species of animal found at Botai sites

(E) analysis of the ratio of human remains to horse remains found in Botai ceremonial sites

GO ON TO THE NEXT PAGE.

Passage A

Music does not always gain by association with words. Like images, words can excite the deepest emotions but are inadequate to express the emotions they excite. Music is more adequate, and hence will
(5) often seize an emotion that may have been excited by images or words, deepen its expression, and, by so doing, excite still deeper emotion. That is how words can gain by being set to music.

But to set words to music—as in opera or song—
(10) is in fact to mix two arts together. A striking effect may be produced, but at the expense of the purity of each art. Poetry is a great art; so is music. But as a medium for emotion, each is greater alone than in company, although various good ends arise from
(15) linking the two, providing that the words are subordinated to the more expressive medium of music. What good could any words do for Beethoven's *Fifth Symphony*? So too an opera is largely independent of words, and depends for its aesthetic value not upon the
(20) poetry of the libretto (the words of the opera), or even the plot or scenery, but upon its emotional range—a region dominated by the musical element.

Passage B

Throughout the history of opera, two fundamental types may be distinguished: that in which the music is
(25) primary, and that in which there is, essentially, parity between music and other factors. The former, sometimes called "singer's opera"—a term which has earned undeserved contempt—is exemplified by most Italian operas, while the latter, exemplified by the
(30) operas of German composer Richard Wagner, depend for their effect on a balance among many factors of which music is only one, albeit the most important. Theoretically, it would seem that there should be a third kind of opera, in which the music is subordinated
(35) to the other features. While the earliest operas were of this kind, their appeal was limited, and a fuller participation of music was required to establish opera on a secure basis.

In any event, in any aesthetic judgment of opera,
(40) regardless of the opera's type, neither the music nor the poetry of the libretto should be judged in isolation. The music is good not if it would make a good concert piece but if it serves the particular situation in the opera in which it occurs, contributing something not
(45) supplied by other elements. Similarly, the poetry is good not because it reads well by itself but primarily if, while embodying a sound dramatic idea, it furnishes opportunity for effective musical and scenic treatment. True, the elements of music and poetry may be
(50) considered separately, but only for purposes of analyzing their formal features. In actuality these elements are as united as hydrogen and oxygen are united in water. It is this union—further enriched and clarified by the visual action—that results in opera's
(55) inimitable character.

15. The authors of both passages attempt to answer which one of the following questions?

   (A) Is music inherently a more expressive medium than poetry?
   (B) Is the emotive power of poetry enhanced when it is set to music?
   (C) Should opera be accorded the same respect as other forms of classical music?
   (D) How important are words to the artistic effectiveness of opera?
   (E) How is opera different from all other musical art forms?

16. Which one of the following issues is addressed by the author of passage A but not by the author of passage B?

   (A) the importance of music to any aesthetic judgment of an operatic work
   (B) how music is affected when it is combined with words
   (C) the ability of music to evoke an emotional response in the listener
   (D) whether music should ever be subordinated to words with which it is combined
   (E) whether music should be judged in isolation from the libretto in opera

17. Passage B, but not passage A, includes which one of the following topics in its discussion of opera?

   (A) the importance of plot and scenery to an opera's aesthetic value
   (B) the ability of images and words to excite deep emotion
   (C) the consequences of combining poetry and music into a single art form
   (D) the relative roles of music and libretto in opera
   (E) the differences among different types of opera

GO ON TO THE NEXT PAGE.

18. It can be inferred that the author of passage B has which one of the following opinions of opera in which the words are subordinated to the music?

    (A)   It is primarily a popular art form.
    (B)   It has been justly criticized for betraying opera's main objectives.
    (C)   It is emotionally more expressive than other types of opera.
    (D)   It is as legitimate as other types of opera.
    (E)   It should be judged as though it were a concert piece.

19. Which one of the following is a principle that is implicit in the argument made by the author of passage B but that would most likely be rejected by the author of passage A?

    (A)   An opera's nonmusical elements are essential to the opera's aesthetic value.
    (B)   Even in operas where there is relative parity among the various elements, the music is the most important element.
    (C)   An opera cannot be artistically successful unless it skillfully balances many factors.
    (D)   In order for an opera to be artistically successful, the music should not be subordinated to other features of the opera.
    (E)   An opera's libretto has formal features that can be analyzed independently of the opera's music.

20. The author of passage B defines a "singer's opera" as an opera

    (A)   in which there is relative parity between the music and other elements
    (B)   in which the drama is of paramount importance
    (C)   that is generally of lower artistic merit
    (D)   from the art form's earliest historical period
    (E)   in which nonmusical elements are subordinate

21. The author of passage A would be most likely to regard the discussion in passage B regarding "a third kind of opera" (lines 33–38) as evidence of which one of the following propositions?

    (A)   Both poetry and music are diminished by being joined in one art form.
    (B)   The aesthetic value of an opera depends largely on the quality of its music.
    (C)   The musical and nonmusical elements of opera are indivisible from one another.
    (D)   Music invariably gains by being combined with poetry.
    (E)   Opera requires the careful balancing of many competing but equal elements.

GO ON TO THE NEXT PAGE.

According to the generally accepted theory of plate tectonics, the earth's crust consists of a dozen or so plates of solid rock moving across the mantle—the slightly fluid layer of rock between crust and core.

(5) Most earthquakes can then be explained as a result of the grinding of these plates against one another as they collide. When two plates collide, one plate is forced under the other until it eventually merges with the underlying mantle. According to this explanation, this

(10) process, called subduction, causes an enormous build-up of energy that is abruptly released in the form of an earthquake. Most earthquakes take place in the earth's seismic "hot zones"—regions with very high levels of subduction. Contrary to expectations,

(15) however, global seismic data indicate that there are also regions with high levels of subduction that are nonetheless nearly free of earthquakes. Thus, until recently, there remained a crucial question for which the plate tectonics theory had no answer—how can

(20) often intense subduction take place at certain locations with little or no seismic effect?

One group of scientists now proposes that the relative quiet of these zones is tied to the nature of the collision between the plates. In many seismic hot zones,

(25) the plates exhibit motion in opposite directions— that is, they collide because they are moving toward each other. And because the two plates are moving in opposite directions, the subduction zone is relatively motionless relative to the underlying mantle. In

(30) contrast, the plate collisions in the quiet subduction zones occur between two plates that are moving in the same general direction—the second plate's motion is simply faster than that of the first, and its leading edge therefore becomes subducted. But in this type of

(35) subduction, the collision zone moves with a comparatively high velocity relative to the mantle below. Thus, rather like an oar dipped into the water from a moving boat, the overtaking plate encounters great resistance from the mantle and is forced to

(40) descend steeply as it is absorbed into the mantle. The steep descent of the overtaking plate in this type of collision reduces the amount of contact between the two plates, and the earthquake-producing friction is thereby reduced as well. On the other hand, in

(45) collisions in which the plates move toward each other the subducted plate receives relatively little resistance from the mantle, and so its angle of descent is correspondingly shallow, allowing for a much larger plane of contact between the two plates. Like two

(50) sheets of sandpaper pressed together, these plates offer each other a great deal of resistance.

This proposal also provides a warning. It suggests that regions that were previously thought to be seismically innocuous—regions with low levels of

(55) subduction—may in fact be at a significant risk of earthquakes, depending on the nature of the subduction taking place.

22. Which one of the following most accurately expresses the main point of the passage?

(A) As a result of differences in resistance when colliding plates are moving in the same or in opposite directions, the amount of subduction in a region is strongly correlated with the number of earthquakes.

(B) The differences between how colliding plates interact when moving in the same or in opposite directions offer scientists a plausible explanation of the rarity of earthquakes in some regions of intense subduction.

(C) Some scientists theorize that seismic "quiet zones" with almost no earthquakes occur where plates are traveling in the same direction and, consequently, do not collide with each other.

(D) A new version of the theory of plate tectonics that abandons the generally accepted explanation of earthquakes as resulting from the process of subduction has been posited by some scientists.

(E) The generally accepted theory of plate tectonics is threatened by new evidence that there are regions of the earth with high levels of subduction but which, nevertheless, have relatively low levels of seismic activity.

23. According to the passage, what results when two plates moving in the same direction collide?

(A) The trailing edge of the slower-moving plate is subducted under the faster-moving plate.

(B) The leading edge of the slower-moving plate is subducted under the faster-moving plate.

(C) The trailing edge of the faster-moving plate is subducted under the slower-moving plate.

(D) The leading edge of the faster-moving plate is subducted under the slower-moving plate.

(E) The leading edge of the smaller plate is subducted under the larger plate.

GO ON TO THE NEXT PAGE.

24. Which one of the following, if true, would present the greatest challenge to the new proposal relating the amount of seismic activity to the type of collision between tectonic plates?

    (A) Some regions where seismic activity is infrequent but subduction regularly occurs are regions in which the colliding plates move across the mantle in the same direction.

    (B) There are areas in which plates collide but in which there is little or no seismic activity.

    (C) There are areas where a plate has descended at a shallow angle during subduction but where there have been few, if any, earthquakes.

    (D) The size of the plane of contact between colliding plates is related only to the angle at which subduction occurs.

    (E) There is an area where a plate descended at a steep angle during subduction but there has been little or no seismic activity.

25. Based on the information in the passage, which one of the following sentences would most logically complete the last paragraph?

    (A) Depending on the relationship between plate velocity and mantle, there is always the possibility that plate velocity could increase.

    (B) The lower the level of subduction in an area, the greater the probability that any subduction there is occurring at a shallow angle.

    (C) Any region where subduction occurs could suffer an increase in the level of subduction and a consequent increase in seismic activity.

    (D) Even at low levels, the process known as subduction inevitably results in a significant amount of seismic activity.

    (E) Even in such a region, a plate descending at a shallow angle is likely to cause a great deal of earthquake-producing friction.

26. According to the information in the passage, which one of the following kinds of regions experiences the most earthquakes?

    (A) regions where the nature of the collision between plates is such that one plate descends sharply into the mantle

    (B) regions where resistance from the mantle during subduction is greatest

    (C) regions where subduction occurs at shallow angles

    (D) regions where there is the greatest amount of subduction

    (E) regions where plates are traveling in the same general direction

27. Which one of the following statements regarding seismic activity can be inferred from the passage?

    (A) Earthquakes are frequent in any zones where there is considerable motion of colliding plates in relation to the underlying mantle.

    (B) Earthquakes are equally likely to occur at any point along the plane of contact between two colliding plates.

    (C) Seismic quiet zones are at particular risk due to the very gradual accumulation of energy, which gets released relatively infrequently.

    (D) No region can be identified as a subduction zone unless earthquakes occur there.

    (E) Earthquakes are more likely to result where there is a large plane of contact between plates during subduction.

S T O P

IF YOU FINISH BEFORE TIME IS CALLED, YOU MAY CHECK YOUR WORK ON THIS SECTION ONLY.
DO NOT WORK ON ANY OTHER SECTION IN THE TEST.

SECTION II

Time—35 minutes

26 Questions

<u>Directions</u>: Each question in this section is based on the reasoning presented in a brief passage. In answering the questions, you should not make assumptions that are by commonsense standards implausible, superfluous, or incompatible with the passage. For some questions, more than one of the choices could conceivably answer the question. However, you are to choose the <u>best</u> answer; that is, choose the response that most accurately and completely answers the question and mark that response on your answer sheet.

1. Ullman: Plato argued that because of the harmful ways in which music can manipulate the emotions, societies need to put restrictions on the music their citizens hear. However, because musicians seek not to manipulate the emotions but to create beauty, this argument is misguided.

Ullman's argument is most vulnerable to criticism on the grounds that it fails to consider the possibility that

(A)   what musicians intend their music to do and what it actually does are different
(B)   those with the power to censor music would not censor other forms of expression
(C)   there are other, more convincing arguments for allowing the censorship of music
(D)   other forms of art have more potential to be harmful to society than music has
(E)   artists who are trying to manipulate people's emotions to control them are not likely to admit it

2. Physician: A tax on saturated fat, which was intended to reduce consumption of unhealthy foods, has been repealed after having been in effect for only seven months. The tax was apparently having some undesirable and unintended consequences, encouraging people to travel to neighboring countries to purchase certain foods, for example. Nonetheless, the tax should not have been repealed so soon.

Which one of the following principles, if valid, most helps to justify the physician's conclusion regarding the tax?

(A)   A tax on unhealthy foods should be implemented only if it can be known with a high degree of certainty that it will actually improve people's health.
(B)   It is not possible to adequately gauge the impact of a tax intended to affect people's health until the tax has been in effect for at least one year.
(C)   Before any law intended to improve people's health is implemented, all foreseeable negative consequences should be carefully considered.
(D)   A law intended to improve people's health should be repealed if it is clear that most people are evading the law.
(E)   A tax on unhealthy foods should be applied only to those foods that are widely believed to be the most unhealthy.

3. Legislator: A foreign company is attempting to buy FerroMetal, a domestic iron-mining company. We should prohibit this sale. Since manufacturing is central to our economy, we need a dependable supply of iron ore. If we allow a foreign company to buy FerroMetal, we will have no grounds to stop foreign companies from buying other iron-mining companies. Soon foreigners will control most of the iron mining here, leaving our manufacturers at their mercy. The end result will be that our manufacturers will no longer be able to rely on a domestic supply of iron ore.

Which one of the following most accurately describes a flaw in the reasoning of the legislator's argument?

(A)   The argument draws a conclusion that simply restates a premise presented in support of that conclusion.
(B)   The argument takes for granted that what is true of one particular industry is true of industry in general.
(C)   The argument defends a practice solely on the grounds that the practice is widely accepted.
(D)   The argument presents a chain of possible consequences of a given event as if it were the only possible chain of consequences of that event.
(E)   The argument concludes that one event would cause a second event even though the second event would have to precede the first.

GO ON TO THE NEXT PAGE.

4. Food company engineer: I stand by my decision to order the dumping of small amounts of chemicals into the local river even though there is some evidence that this material may pose health problems. I fish in the river myself and will continue to do so. Furthermore, I will have no problem if other food manufacturers do what our company does.

The engineer's reasoning most closely conforms to which one of the following principles?

(A) One is justified in performing an act if other people are also planning to perform that kind of act.

(B) One should always choose to act in a way that will benefit the greatest number of people.

(C) One is justified in performing an act if one is willing to submit oneself to the consequences of that action performed by oneself or others.

(D) One should never perform an act until one has fully analyzed all the ways in which that act could impact others.

(E) One has the right to perform an act as long as that act does not harm anyone else.

5. Political strategist: Clearly, attacking an opposing candidate on philosophical grounds is generally more effective than attacking the details of the opponent's policy proposals. A philosophical attack links an opponent's policy proposals to an overarching ideological scheme, thereby telling a story and providing context. This makes the attack emotionally compelling.

Which one of the following is an assumption required by the political strategist's argument?

(A) The stories that people are most likely to remember are those that are emotionally compelling.

(B) Political attacks that are emotionally compelling are generally more effective than those that are not.

(C) Political attacks that tell a story are able to provide more context than those that do not.

(D) Voters are typically uninterested in the details of candidates' policy proposals.

(E) Most candidates' policy proposals are grounded in an overarching ideological scheme.

6. Michaela: I think doctors who complain about patients doing medical research on the Internet are being a little unfair. It seems only natural that a patient would want to know as much as possible about his or her condition.

Sam: It is not unfair. Doctors have undergone years of training. How can you maintain that a doctor's opinion is not worth more than something an untrained person comes up with after searching the Internet?

Sam's response indicates that he interpreted Michaela's remarks to mean that

(A) health information found on the Internet is trustworthy

(B) the opinion of a patient who has done Internet research on his or her condition should have at least as much weight as the opinion of a doctor

(C) the opinion of a patient's own doctor should not be given more weight than the opinions of doctors published on websites

(D) a doctor's explanation of a patient's symptoms should be taken more seriously than the patient's own view of his or her symptoms

(E) patients who do not research their conditions on the Internet give their doctors' opinions more consideration

7. Principle: People should not feed wild animals because it makes them dependent on humans and less likely to survive on their own.

Situation: Bird lovers commonly feed wild birds to attract them to their yards and gardens.

Which one of the following, if assumed, would most help to justify treating the human feeding of wild birds as an exception to the principle above?

(A) Congregating around human bird feeders makes wild birds more vulnerable to predators and diseases.

(B) Some species of wild birds benefit humans by consuming large numbers of mosquitoes and other insect pests.

(C) Wild birds are much more likely to congregate in yards where they are fed than in yards where they are not fed.

(D) Most bird lovers are very active in efforts to preserve the habitats of threatened species of wild birds and other animals.

(E) Human settlement is so pervasive in the habitat of most wild birds that they must depend in part on human sources of food for survival.

GO ON TO THE NEXT PAGE.

8. Normally, political candidates send out campaign material in order to influence popular opinion. But the recent ads for Ebsen's campaign were sent to too few households to serve this purpose effectively. The ads were evidently sent out to test their potential to influence popular opinion. They covered a wide variety of topics, and Ebsen's campaign has been spending heavily on follow-up to gauge their effect on recipients.

Which one of the following most accurately expresses the conclusion drawn in the argument above?

(A) Normally, political candidates send out campaign material to influence popular opinion.

(B) The recent ads for Ebsen's campaign were sent to too few households to influence popular opinion effectively.

(C) The recent ads for Ebsen's campaign were sent out to test their potential to influence popular opinion.

(D) The recent ads for Ebsen's campaign covered a wide variety of topics.

(E) Ebsen's campaign has been spending heavily on follow-up surveys to gauge the ads' effect on recipients.

9. Last year, pharmaceutical manufacturers significantly increased the amount of money they spent promoting new drugs, which they do mainly by sending sales representatives to visit physicians in their offices. However, two years ago there was an average of 640 such visits per representative, whereas last year that figure fell to 501. So the additional promotion must have been counterproductive, making physicians less willing to receive visits by pharmaceutical sales representatives.

Which one of the following, if true, most weakens the argument?

(A) Most pharmaceutical manufacturers increased the size of their sales forces so that their sales representatives could devote more time to each physician.

(B) Physicians who receive visits from pharmaceutical sales representatives usually accept free samples of medication from the representatives' companies.

(C) Most pharmaceutical companies did not increase the amount of money they spend promoting drugs through advertising targeted directly at consumers.

(D) Most physicians who agree to receive a visit from a pharmaceutical sales representative will see that representative more than once during a given year.

(E) The more visits a physician receives from a pharmaceutical sales representative, the more likely he or she is to prescribe drugs made by that representative's company.

10. Archaeologist: The extensive network of ancient tracks on the island of Malta was most likely created through erosion caused by the passage of wheeled vehicles. Some researchers have suggested that the tracks were in fact manually cut to facilitate the passage of carts, citing the uniformity in track depth. However, this uniformity is more likely indicative of wheel diameter: Routes were utilized until tracks eroded to a depth that made vehicle passage impossible.

Which one of the following is the overall conclusion of the archaeologist's argument?

(A) The extensive network of ancient tracks on the island of Malta was most likely created through erosion caused by the passage of wheeled vehicles.

(B) Some researchers have suggested that the ancient tracks on the island of Malta were in fact manually cut to facilitate the passage of carts.

(C) Some researchers cite the uniformity of the depth of the ancient tracks on the island of Malta to support the suggestion that they were manually cut.

(D) The uniformity of depth of the ancient tracks on the island of Malta is probably indicative of the wheel diameter of the carts that passed over them.

(E) The ancient tracks on the island of Malta were utilized until they eroded to a depth that made vehicle passage impossible.

11. The goal of reforesting degraded land is to create an area with a multitude of thriving tree species. But some experienced land managers use a reforesting strategy that involves planting a single fast-growing tree species.

Which one of the following, if true, most helps to resolve the apparent discrepancy in the information above?

(A) Tree species that require abundant sunlight tend to grow quickly on degraded land.

(B) An area with a multitude of thriving tree species tends to be more aesthetically pleasing than an area with only a single tree species.

(C) The reforestation of degraded land is generally unsuccessful unless the land is planted with tree species that are native to the area designated for reforestation.

(D) The growth of trees attracts wildlife whose activities contribute to the dispersal of a large variety of tree seeds from surrounding areas.

(E) The process of reforesting degraded sites is time consuming and labor intensive.

GO ON TO THE NEXT PAGE.

12. An independent computer service company tallied the service requests it receives for individual brands of personal computers. It found that, after factoring in each brand's market share, KRV brand computers had the largest proportion of service requests, whereas ProBit brand computers had the smallest proportion of service requests. Obviously, ProBit is the more reliable personal computer brand.

Which one of the following, if true, most seriously weakens the argument?

(A) The proportions of service requests for the other computer brands in the tally were clustered much closer to the ProBit level of service requests than to the KRV level.

(B) For some computer brands, but not for others, most service requests are made to the manufacturer's service department rather than to an independent service company.

(C) The company that did the tally receives more service requests for ProBit brand computers than does any other independent computer service company.

(D) The computer brands covered in the computer service company's tally differ greatly with respect to their market share.

(E) ProBit has been selling personal computers for many more years than has KRV.

13. When scientific journals began to offer full online access to their articles in addition to the traditional printed volumes, scientists gained access to more journals and easier access to back issues. Surprisingly, this did not lead to a broader variety of articles being cited in new scientific articles. Instead, it led to a greater tendency among scientists to cite the same articles that their fellow scientists cited.

Which one of the following, if true, most helps to explain the surprising outcome described above?

(A) A few of the most authoritative scientific journals were among the first to offer full online access to their articles.

(B) Scientists who wrote a lot of articles were the most enthusiastic about accessing journal articles online.

(C) Scientists are more likely to cite articles by scientists that they know than they are to cite articles by scientists they have never met, even if the latter are more prominent.

(D) Several new scientific journals appeared at roughly the same time that full online access to scientific articles became commonplace.

(E) Online searching made it easier for scientists to identify the articles that present the most highly regarded views on an issue, which they prefer to cite.

14. Researcher: People are able to tell whether a person is extroverted just by looking at pictures in which the person has a neutral expression. Since people are also able to tell whether a chimpanzee behaves dominantly just by looking at a picture of the chimpanzee's expressionless face, and since both humans and chimpanzees are primates, we conclude that this ability is probably not acquired solely through culture but rather as a result of primate biology.

Which one of the following, if true, most strengthens the researcher's argument?

(A) People are generally unable to judge the dominance of bonobos, which are also primates, by looking at pictures of them.

(B) People are able to identify a wider range of personality traits from pictures of other people than from pictures of chimpanzees.

(C) Extroversion in people and dominant behavior in chimpanzees are both indicators of a genetic predisposition to assertiveness.

(D) Any common ancestor of humans and chimpanzees would have to have lived over 7 million years ago.

(E) Some of the pictures of people used in the experiments were composites of several different people.

15. All the apartments on 20th Avenue are in old houses. However, there are twice as many apartments on 20th Avenue as there are old houses. Therefore, most old houses on 20th Avenue contain more than one apartment.

The reasoning in the argument above is most vulnerable to criticism on the grounds that the argument

(A) overlooks the possibility that some of the buildings on 20th Avenue are not old houses

(B) draws a conclusion that simply restates one of the premises offered in support of the conclusion

(C) fails to consider the possibility that some buildings on 20th Avenue may offer types of rental accommodation other than apartments

(D) confuses a condition whose presence would be sufficient to ensure the truth of the argument's conclusion with a condition whose presence is required in order for the conclusion to be true

(E) fails to address the possibility that a significant number of old houses on 20th Avenue contain three or more apartments

GO ON TO THE NEXT PAGE.

16. Scientist: An orbiting spacecraft detected a short-term spike in sulfur dioxide in Venus's atmosphere. Volcanoes are known to cause sulfur dioxide spikes in Earth's atmosphere, and Venus has hundreds of mountains that show signs of past volcanic activity. But we should not conclude that volcanic activity caused the spike on Venus. No active volcanoes have been identified on Venus, and planetary atmospheres are known to undergo some cyclical variations in chemical composition.

Which one of the following, if true, most weakens the scientist's argument?

(A) Conditions on Venus make it unlikely that any instrument targeting Venus would detect a volcanic eruption directly.

(B) Evidence suggests that there was a short-term spike in sulfur dioxide in Venus's atmosphere 30 years earlier.

(C) Levels of sulfur dioxide have been higher in Venus's atmosphere than in Earth's atmosphere over the long term.

(D) Traces of the sulfur dioxide from volcanic eruptions on Earth are detectable in the atmosphere years after the eruptions take place.

(E) Most instances of sulfur dioxide spikes in the Earth's atmosphere are caused by the burning of fossil fuels.

17. Increasing the electrical load carried on a transmission line increases the line's temperature, and too great a load will cause the line to exceed its maximum operating temperature. The line's temperature is also affected by wind speed and direction: Strong winds cool the line more than light winds, and wind blowing across a line cools it more than does wind blowing parallel to it.

Which one of the following is most strongly supported by the information above?

(A) Electrical utility companies typically increase the electrical load on their transmission lines on days on which the wind has a strong cooling effect.

(B) Transmission lines that run parallel to the prevailing winds can generally carry greater electrical loads than otherwise identical lines at a right angle to the prevailing winds.

(C) The electrical load that a transmission line can carry without reaching its maximum operating temperature increases when the wind speed increases.

(D) Air temperature has less effect on the temperature of a transmission line than wind speed does.

(E) The maximum operating temperature of a transmission line is greater on windy days than on calm days.

18. In grasslands near the Namib Desert there are "fairy circles"—large, circular patches that are entirely devoid of vegetation. Since sand termite colonies were found in every fairy circle they investigated, scientists hypothesize that it is the burrowing activities of these termites that cause the circles to form.

Which one of the following, if true, most supports the scientists' hypothesis?

(A) Dying grass plants within newly forming fairy circles are damaged only at the roots.

(B) The grasses that grow around fairy circles are able to survive even the harshest and most prolonged droughts in the region.

(C) The soil in fairy circles typically has higher water content than the soil in areas immediately outside the circles.

(D) Fairy circles tend to form in areas that already have numerous other fairy circles.

(E) Species of animals that feed on sand termites are often found living near fairy circles.

GO ON TO THE NEXT PAGE.

19. Munroe was elected in a landslide. It is impossible for Munroe to have been elected without both a fundamental shift in the sentiments of the electorate and a well-run campaign. Thus, one cannot avoid the conclusion that there has been a fundamental shift in the sentiments of the electorate.

Which one of the following arguments is most closely parallel in its reasoning to the argument above?

(A) The Park Street Cafe closed this year even though its customer base was satisfied. So, because its customer base was satisfied, the only conclusion one can draw is that the Park Street Cafe closed because it was facing strong competition.

(B) The Park Street Cafe closed this year. So we must conclude that the Park Street Cafe was facing strong competition, since it would not have closed unless it was true both that it was facing strong competition and that its customer base was unsatisfied.

(C) No one can argue that the Park Street Cafe closed this year because its customer base was not satisfied. Even if its customer base was not satisfied, the Park Street Cafe would have closed only if it was facing strong competition.

(D) The Park Street Cafe closed this year. There was no reason for it to remain open if it was facing strong competition and had an unsatisfied customer base. So one cannot rule out the possibility that it was both facing strong competition and had an unsatisfied customer base.

(E) The Park Street Cafe closed this year. In order to stay open, it needed a lack of competition and it needed a satisfied customer base. Because it had neither, the unavoidable conclusion is that the Park Street Cafe could not have stayed open this year.

20. For pollinating certain crops such as cranberries, bumblebees are far more efficient than honeybees. This is because a bumblebee tends to visit only a few plant species in a limited area, whereas a honeybee generally flies over a much broader area and visits a wider variety of species.

Which one of the following is most strongly supported by the information above?

(A) If a honeybee visits a wider variety of plant species than a bumblebee visits, the honeybee will be less efficient than the bumblebee at pollinating any one of those species.

(B) The number of plant species other than cranberries that a bee visits affects the efficiency with which the bee pollinates cranberries.

(C) The broader an area a bee flies over, the smaller the number of plant species that bee will be able to visit.

(D) Cranberries are typically found concentrated in limited areas that bumblebees are more likely than honeybees ever to visit.

(E) The greater the likelihood of a given bee species visiting one or more plants in a given cranberry crop, the more efficient that bee species will be at pollinating that crop.

21. Economist: Currently the interest rates that banks pay to borrow are higher than the interest rates that they can receive for loans to large, financially strong companies. Banks will not currently lend to companies that are not financially strong, and total lending by banks to small and medium-sized companies is less than it was five years ago. So total bank lending to companies is less than it was five years ago.

The economist's conclusion follows logically if which one of the following is assumed?

(A) Banks will not lend money at interest rates that are lower than the interest rates they pay to borrow.

(B) Most small and medium-sized companies were financially stronger five years ago than they are now.

(C) Five years ago, some banks would lend to companies that were not financially strong.

(D) The interest rates that banks currently pay to borrow are higher than the rates they paid five years ago.

(E) The interest rates that small and medium-sized companies pay to borrow are higher than those paid by large, financially strong companies.

GO ON TO THE NEXT PAGE.

22. Counselor: To be kind to someone, one must want that person to prosper. Yet, even two people who dislike each other may nevertheless treat each other with respect. And while no two people who dislike each other can be fully content in each other's presence, any two people who do not dislike each other will be kind to each other.

If the counselor's statements are true, then which one of the following must be false?

(A) Some people who like each other are not fully content in each other's presence.

(B) Some people who are fully content in each other's presence do not want each other to prosper.

(C) Some people who treat each other with respect are not fully content in each other's presence.

(D) Some people who want each other to prosper dislike each other.

(E) Some people who are kind to each other do not treat each other with respect.

23. A gram of the artificial sweetener aspartame is much sweeter than a gram of sugar. Soft drinks that are sweetened with sugar are, of course, sweet, so those sweetened with aspartame must be even sweeter. Thus people who regularly drink soft drinks sweetened with aspartame will develop a preference for extremely sweet products.

Which one of the following arguments exhibits flawed reasoning that is most similar to flawed reasoning in the argument above?

(A) People sometimes develop a preference for foods that they initially disliked. So if you dislike a new food, then you will eventually develop a preference for it.

(B) Most people own more books than televisions. Moreover, it takes longer to read a book than to watch an episode of a television show. So most people must spend more time reading than they do watching television.

(C) Joe's piggy bank has only pennies in it, and Maria's has only nickels. Nickels are worth much more than pennies. It therefore follows that there is more money in Maria's piggy bank than in Joe's.

(D) Stephanie likes hot summer weather much more than Katherine does. So the place where Stephanie grew up must have had more days of hot summer weather than the place where Katherine grew up.

(E) Guillermo has a much shorter drive to work than Abdul does. So Guillermo's estimate of the average commute for workers in the country as a whole is likely to be lower than Abdul's estimate.

24. Economist: If minimum wage levels are low, employers have a greater incentive to hire more workers than to buy productivity-enhancing new technology. As a result, productivity growth, which is necessary for higher average living standards, falls off. Conversely, high minimum wage levels result in higher productivity. Thus, raising our currently low minimum wage levels would improve the country's overall economic health more than any hiring cutbacks triggered by the raise would harm it.

Which one of the following, if true, most strengthens the economist's argument?

(A) Productivity growth in a country usually leads to an eventual increase in job creation.

(B) The economist's country has seen a slow but steady increase in its unemployment rate over the last decade.

(C) A country's unemployment rate is a key factor in determining its average living standards.

(D) The economist's country currently lags behind other countries in the development of new technology.

(E) Productivity-enhancing new technology tends to quickly become outdated.

GO ON TO THE NEXT PAGE.

25. Mayor: Periodically an ice cream company will hold a free ice cream day as a promotion. Showing up may not cost you any money, but it sure does cost you time. We learn from this that when something valuable costs no money you get overconsumption and long lines. Currently, those who drive to work complain about the congestion they face in their rush-hour commutes. What is needed is a system for charging people for the use of roads during rush hour. Then rush hour congestion will abate.

The claim that when something valuable costs no money you get overconsumption and long lines plays which one of the following roles in the mayor's argument?

(A) It is a hypothesis that is rejected in favor of the hypothesis stated in the argument's overall conclusion.

(B) It is a concession made to those who dispute an analogy drawn in the argument.

(C) It helps establish the importance of the argument's overall conclusion, but is not offered as evidence for that conclusion.

(D) It is a general claim used in support of the argument's overall conclusion.

(E) It is the overall conclusion of the argument.

26. The advertising campaign for Roadwise auto insurance is notable for the variety of its commercials, which range from straightforward and informative to funny and offbeat. This is unusual in the advertising world, where companies typically strive for uniformity in advertising in order to establish a brand identity with their target demographic. But in this case variety is a smart approach, since purchasers of auto insurance are so demographically diverse.

Which one of the following, if true, adds the most support for the conclusion of the argument?

(A) Advertising campaigns designed to target one demographic sometimes appeal to a wider group of people than expected.

(B) Consistent efforts to establish a brand identity are critical for encouraging product interest and improving company recognition.

(C) Fewer people are influenced by auto insurance commercials than by commercials for other types of products.

(D) Advertising campaigns that target one demographic often alienate people who are not part of the target demographic.

(E) Efforts to influence a target demographic do not pay off when the content of the advertising campaign falls short.

S T O P

IF YOU FINISH BEFORE TIME IS CALLED, YOU MAY CHECK YOUR WORK ON THIS SECTION ONLY.
DO NOT WORK ON ANY OTHER SECTION IN THE TEST.

SECTION III
Time—35 minutes
25 Questions

Directions: Each question in this section is based on the reasoning presented in a brief passage. In answering the questions, you should not make assumptions that are by commonsense standards implausible, superfluous, or incompatible with the passage. For some questions, more than one of the choices could conceivably answer the question. However, you are to choose the best answer; that is, choose the response that most accurately and completely answers the question and mark that response on your answer sheet.

1. Researchers put two electrodes in a pool that a dolphin swam in. When the dolphin swam near the electrodes, the researchers would sometimes create a weak electric field by activating the electrodes. The dolphin would swim away if the electrodes were activated; otherwise it acted normally. The researchers then placed a plastic shield over small organs called vibrissal crypts located on the dolphin's snout. With the crypts covered, the dolphin no longer swam away when the electrodes were activated.

The statements above, if true, most strongly support which one of the following?

(A) In the wild, dolphins sometimes encounter strong electric fields.
(B) Vibrissal crypts enable dolphins to sense electric fields.
(C) Dolphins do not instinctually avoid electric fields, but they can be trained to do so.
(D) Electric fields interfere with the normal functioning of dolphins' vibrissal crypts.
(E) Under normal circumstances, dolphins are unable to sense electric fields.

2. In a study of honesty conducted in various retail stores, customers who paid in cash and received change were given an extra dollar with their change. Few people who received an extra dollar returned it. So, among those who received an extra dollar, most behaved dishonestly.

The answer to which one of the following questions would most help in evaluating the argument?

(A) Did those who received an extra dollar count their change?
(B) What percentage of the retail transactions studied were cash transactions?
(C) Would the people who returned the extra dollar describe themselves as honest?
(D) Did the people who returned the extra dollar suspect that it was given to them intentionally?
(E) Does increasing the extra change to five dollars have an effect on people's behavior?

3. Dario: The government should continue to grant patents for all new drug compounds. Patents promote innovation by rewarding pharmaceutical companies for undertaking the costly research needed to develop new drugs.

Cynthia: Promoting innovation is certainly important. For this reason, patents should be granted only for truly innovative drugs, not for minor variants of previously existing drugs. Since it is much less expensive to tweak an existing drug than to develop a wholly new one, pharmaceutical companies tend to focus primarily on the cheaper alternative.

Dario and Cynthia disagree over whether

(A) pharmaceutical companies should be rewarded for pursuing innovation
(B) patents should be granted for all drug compounds
(C) developing truly innovative drugs is costly
(D) pharmaceutical companies have an incentive to create minor variants of existing drugs
(E) drug patents can promote innovation

4. There are only two possible reasons that it would be wrong to engage in an activity that causes pollution: because pollution harms ecosystems, which are valuable in themselves; or, ecosystems aside, because pollution harms human populations. Either way, it would not be wrong to perform mining operations on Mars. Although doing so would pollute Mars, the small human presence needed to run the mining operation would be completely protected from the Martian environment and would suffer no harm.

The conclusion drawn above follows logically if which one of the following is assumed?

(A) Mining creates less pollution than many other human activities.
(B) There are no ecosystems on Mars.
(C) The economic benefits of mining on Mars would outweigh its costs.
(D) It is technologically feasible to perform mining operations on Mars.
(E) The more complex an ecosystem is, the more valuable it is.

GO ON TO THE NEXT PAGE.

5. A person with low self-esteem will be treated disrespectfully more often than will a person with high self-esteem. Moreover, a recent experiment found that, when people with low self-esteem and those with high self-esteem are both confronted with the same treatment by others, people with low self-esteem are much more likely to feel that they have been treated disrespectfully. Thus, _____.

Which one of the following most logically completes the argument?

(A) people with low self-esteem are usually right when they think they have been treated disrespectfully

(B) being treated disrespectfully tends to cause a person to develop lower self-esteem

(C) if an individual has been treated disrespectfully, it is probably because the individual was perceived to have low self-esteem

(D) people with low self-esteem more frequently think that they are being treated disrespectfully than do people with high self-esteem

(E) a person with low self-esteem will be more inclined to treat others disrespectfully than will a person with high self-esteem

6. Watanabe: To protect the native kokanee salmon in the lake, we must allow fishing of native trout. Each mature trout eats about 250 mature kokanee annually.

Lopez: The real problem is mysis shrimp, which were originally introduced into the lake as food for mature kokanee; but mysis eat plankton—young kokanees' food. The young kokanee are starving to death. So eradicating the shrimp is preferable to allowing trout fishing.

Which one of the following principles, if valid, most strongly supports Lopez's conclusion?

(A) Eliminating a non-native species from a habitat in which it threatens a native species is preferable to any other method of protecting the threatened native species.

(B) When trying to protect the food supply of a particular species, it is best to encourage the method that will have the quickest results, all else being equal.

(C) The number of species in a given habitat should not be reduced if at all possible.

(D) No non-native species should be introduced into a habitat unless all the potential effects of that introduction have been considered.

(E) When seeking to increase the population of a given species, it is most important that one preserve the members of the species who are in the prime reproductive stage of their lives.

7. If rational-choice theory is correct, then people act only in ways that they expect will benefit themselves. But this means that rational-choice theory cannot be correct, because plenty of examples exist of people acting in ways that result in no personal benefit whatsoever.

The argument above is most vulnerable to criticism on the grounds that it

(A) assumes as a premise the contention the argument purports to establish

(B) concludes that a theory is false merely on the grounds that the evidence for it is hypothetical

(C) takes for granted that people who are acting in ways that are personally beneficial expected that their actions would be personally beneficial

(D) presumes, without justification, that examples of people acting in ways that are not personally beneficial greatly outnumber examples of people acting in ways that are personally beneficial

(E) fails to consider that people acting in ways that result in no personal benefit may nonetheless have expected that acting in those ways would produce personal benefit

8. Winds, the movement of gases in the atmosphere of a planet, are ultimately due to differences in atmospheric temperature. Winds on Earth are the result of heat from the Sun, but the Sun is much too far away from Jupiter to have any significant impact on the temperature of Jupiter's atmosphere. Nevertheless, on Jupiter winds reach speeds many times those of winds found on Earth.

Which one of the following, if true, most helps to explain the facts cited above about Jupiter and its winds?

(A) Unlike Earth, Jupiter's atmosphere is warmed by the planet's internal heat source.

(B) Jupiter's atmosphere is composed of several gases that are found in Earth's atmosphere only in trace amounts.

(C) Gaseous planets such as Jupiter sometimes have stronger winds than do rocky planets such as Earth.

(D) There are more planets that have winds stronger than Earth's than there are planets that have winds weaker than Earth's.

(E) Planets even farther from the Sun than Jupiter are known to have atmospheric winds.

GO ON TO THE NEXT PAGE.

9. Until recently it was widely believed that only a limited number of species could reproduce through parthenogenesis, reproduction by a female alone. But lately, as interest in the topic has increased, parthenogenesis has been found in a variety of unexpected cases, including sharks and Komodo dragons. So the number of species that can reproduce through parthenogenesis must be increasing.

The reasoning in the argument is most vulnerable to criticism on the grounds that the argument

(A) equates mere interest in a subject with real understanding of that subject

(B) takes for granted that because one thing follows another, the one must have been caused by the other

(C) takes ignorance of the occurrence of something as conclusive evidence that it did not occur

(D) overlooks a crucial difference between two situations that the argument presents as being similar

(E) presumes that because research is new it is, on that basis alone, better than older research

10. Physician: Clinical psychologists who are not also doctors with medical degrees should not be allowed to prescribe psychiatric medications. Training in clinical psychology includes at most a few hundred hours of education in neuroscience, physiology, and pharmacology. In contrast, doctors with medical degrees must receive years of training in these fields before they are allowed to prescribe psychiatric medications.

Which one of the following principles, if valid, would most help to justify the reasoning in the physician's argument?

(A) Clinical psychologists who are also doctors with medical degrees should be allowed to prescribe psychiatric medications.

(B) Doctors without training in clinical psychology should not be allowed to prescribe psychiatric medications.

(C) No one without years of training in neuroscience, physiology, and pharmacology should be allowed to prescribe psychiatric medications.

(D) The training in neuroscience, physiology, and pharmacology required for a medical degree is sufficient for a doctor to be allowed to prescribe psychiatric medications.

(E) Clinical psychologists should receive years of training in neuroscience, physiology, and pharmacology.

11. Lobbyist: Those who claim that automobile exhaust emissions are a risk to public health are mistaken. During the last century, as automobile exhaust emissions increased, every relevant indicator of public health improved dramatically rather than deteriorated.

The flaw in the lobbyist's reasoning can most effectively be demonstrated by noting that, by parallel reasoning, we could conclude that

(A) inspecting commercial airplanes for safety is unnecessary because the number of commercial airplane crashes has decreased over the last decade

(B) smoking cigarettes is not bad for one's health because not all cigarette smokers get smoking-related illnesses

(C) using a cell phone while driving is not dangerous because the number of traffic accidents has decreased since the invention of the cell phone

(D) skydiving is not dangerous because the number of injuries to skydivers has decreased in recent years

(E) people with insurance do not need to lock their doors because if anything is stolen the insurance company will pay to replace it

12. A recently discovered fossil, which is believed by some to come from *Archaeoraptor liaoningensis*, a species of dinosaur, can serve as evidence that birds evolved from dinosaurs only if the entire fossil is from a single animal. However, the fossil is a composite of bones collected from various parts of the discovery site, so it does not provide evidence that birds evolved from dinosaurs.

The conclusion drawn in the argument follows logically if which one of the following is assumed?

(A) The only paleontologists who believe that the entire fossil is from a single animal are those who were already convinced that birds evolved from dinosaurs.

(B) If the fossil is a composite, then it has pieces of more than one animal.

(C) There are other fossils that provide evidence that birds evolved from dinosaurs.

(D) If the entire fossil is from a single animal, then it is a well-preserved specimen.

(E) The fossil was stolen from the discovery site and sold by someone who cared much more about personal profit than about the accuracy of the fossil record.

GO ON TO THE NEXT PAGE.

13. A new screening test has been developed for syndrome Q. Research has shown that the test yields a positive for syndrome Q whenever the person tested has that syndrome. So, since Justine shows positive on the test, she must have syndrome Q.

Which one of the following most accurately describes a flaw in the reasoning in the argument?

(A) It confuses the claim that a subject will test positive when the syndrome is present with the claim that any subject who tests positive has the syndrome.

(B) It makes a general claim regarding the accuracy of the test for syndrome Q without providing adequate scientific justification for that claim.

(C) It fails to adequately distinguish between a person's not having syndrome Q and that person's not testing positive for syndrome Q.

(D) It confuses a claim about the accuracy of a test for syndrome Q in an arbitrary group of individuals with a similar claim about the accuracy of the test for a single individual.

(E) It confuses the test's having no reliable results for the presence of syndrome Q with its having no reliable results for the absence of syndrome Q.

14. Music historian: In the past, radio stations would not play rock songs that were more than three minutes in length. Rock musicians claimed that such commercial barriers limited their creativity, and some critics argue that only since those barriers have been lifted has rock music become artistic. In fact, however, when these barriers were lifted, the standards for song structures broke down and the music became aimless, because the styles from which rock derived were not well suited to songs of extended length.

Which one of the following is most strongly supported by the music historian's claims?

(A) Rock music is not a good outlet for creative musicians who have a great many ideas.

(B) Rock music must borrow from styles more conducive to songs of extended length if it is to become artistic.

(C) Rock music requires more discipline than some other forms of music.

(D) Rock music can sometimes benefit from the existence of commercial barriers rather than being harmed by them.

(E) Rock music is best when it is made by musicians who do not think of themselves as being self-conscious artists.

15. Some food historians conclude that recipes compiled by an ancient Roman named Apicius are a reliable indicator of how wealthy Romans prepared and spiced their food. Since few other recipes from ancient Rome have survived, this conclusion is far too hasty. After all, the recipes of Apicius may have been highly atypical, just like the recipes of many notable modern chefs.

The argument does which one of the following?

(A) It rejects a view held by some food historians solely on the grounds that there is insufficient evidence to support it.

(B) It offers support for a view held by some food historians by providing a modern analogue to that view.

(C) It takes issue with the view of some food historians by providing a modern analogue that purportedly undercuts their view.

(D) It uses a conclusion drawn by some food historians as the basis for a conclusion about a modern analogue.

(E) It tries to bolster a conclusion about the similarity of historical times to modern times by comparing a conclusion drawn by some food historians to a modern analogue.

GO ON TO THE NEXT PAGE.

16. Wood that is waterlogged or desiccated can be preserved for a significant period, but, under normal conditions, wood usually disintegrates within a century or two. For this reason, archaeologists have been unable to find many remains of early wheeled vehicles to examine. However, archaeologists have found small ceramic models of wheeled vehicles made at approximately the same time as those early vehicles. Since these models have been much less susceptible to disintegration than the vehicles themselves, the main evidence regarding early wheeled vehicles has come from these models.

Which one of the following is most strongly supported by the information above?

(A) Most of the small ceramic models of early wheeled vehicles were made by the very individuals who made the vehicles upon which the ceramic vehicles were modeled.

(B) Few, if any, small models of early wheeled vehicles were made of wood or other materials equally susceptible to disintegration under normal conditions.

(C) The individuals who made the early wheeled vehicles were not always aware that wood can be preserved through waterlogging or desiccation.

(D) An artifact will be more difficult for archaeologists to find if it has been preserved through waterlogging or desiccation than if it has been preserved under more normal conditions.

(E) Of the early wheeled vehicles not preserved, more were made of wood than were made of materials no more susceptible to disintegration than are ceramic items.

17. Traditional hatcheries raise fish in featureless environments and subject them to dull routines, whereas new, experimental hatcheries raise fish in visually stimulating environments with varied routines. When released into the wild, fish from the experimental hatcheries are bolder than those from traditional hatcheries in exploring new environments and trying new types of food. Fish raised in the experimental hatcheries, therefore, are more likely to survive after their release.

Which one of the following is an assumption required by the argument?

(A) It is economically feasible for hatchery operators to expose fish to greater visual stimulation and to more varied routines.

(B) The quality of the environments into which hatchery-raised fish are released has little effect on the fish's survival rate.

(C) Some fish raised in traditional hatcheries die because they are too timid in their foraging for food.

(D) Hatchery-raised fish that are released into the wild need to eat many different types of food to survive.

(E) Fish in the wild always live in visually stimulating environments.

GO ON TO THE NEXT PAGE.

18. An analysis of the language in social media messages posted via the Internet determined that, on average, the use of words associated with positive moods is common in the morning, decreases gradually to a low point midafternoon, and then increases sharply throughout the evening. This shows that a person's mood typically starts out happy in the morning, declines during the day, and improves in the evening.

The reasoning in the argument is most vulnerable to criticism on the grounds that the argument overlooks the possibility that

(A) people's overall moods are lowest at the beginning of the workweek and rise later, peaking on the weekend

(B) many people who post social media messages use neither words associated with positive moods nor words associated with negative moods

(C) the frequency in the use of words in social media is not necessarily indicative of the frequency of the use of those words in other forms of communication

(D) the number of social media messages posted in the morning is not significantly different from the number posted in the evening

(E) most of the social media messages posted in the evening are posted by people who rarely post such messages in the morning

19. Economist: The wages of many of the lowest-paid corporate employees in this country would be protected from cuts by enacting a maximum wage law that prohibits executives at any corporation from earning more than, say, 50 times what the corporation's lowest-paid employees in this country earn. Currently, some executives try to increase corporate profits—and their own salaries—by cutting the pay and benefits of their corporations' employees. A maximum wage law would remove this incentive for these executives to cut the wages of their lowest-paid employees.

Which one of the following is an assumption the economist's argument requires?

(A) All of the lowest-paid corporate employees in the economist's country are employed at corporations at which the executives earn more than 50 times what the corporations' lowest-paid employees in the economist's country earn.

(B) Some corporate executives who cut the pay of their corporations' lowest-paid employees in the economist's country in order to increase their own salaries already earn less than 50 times what their corporations' lowest-paid employees in the economist's country earn.

(C) No corporate executives in the economist's country would raise the wages of their corporations' lowest-paid employees in the economist's country unless such a maximum wage law linked executive wages to those of their corporations' lowest-paid employees in the economist's country.

(D) If corporate executives could not increase their own salaries by cutting the pay and benefits of their corporations' lowest-paid employees in the economist's country, they would never change the wages of those employees.

(E) If such a maximum wage law were enacted in the economist's country, one or more corporate executives would not cut the pay and benefits of their corporations' lowest-paid employees in the economist's country.

GO ON TO THE NEXT PAGE.

20. The level of triglycerides in the blood rises when triglycerides are inadequately metabolized. Research shows that patients with blood triglyceride levels above 1 milligram per milliliter are twice as prone to heart attacks as others. Thus, it is likely that consuming large amounts of fat, processed sugar, or alcohol, each known to increase triglyceride levels in the blood, is a factor causing heart disease.

Which one of the following, if true, most weakens the argument?

(A) People with a high-fat diet who engage in regular, vigorous physical activity are much less likely to develop heart disease than are sedentary people with a low-fat diet.

(B) Triglyceride levels above 2 milligrams per milliliter increase the risk of some serious illnesses not related to heart disease.

(C) Shortly after a person ceases to regularly consume alcohol and processed sugar, that person's triglyceride levels drop dramatically.

(D) Heart disease interferes with the body's ability to metabolize triglycerides.

(E) People who maintain strict regimens for their health tend to adopt low-fat diets and to avoid alcohol and processed sugar.

21. In an experiment, some volunteers were assigned to take aerobics classes and others to take weight-training classes. After three months, each performed an arduous mathematical calculation. Just after that challenge, the measurable stress symptoms of the volunteers in the aerobics classes were less than those of the volunteers in the weight-training classes. This provides good evidence that aerobic exercise helps the body handle psychological stress.

Which one of the following is an assumption the argument requires?

(A) Three months is enough time for the body to fully benefit from aerobic exercise.

(B) The volunteers who were assigned to the aerobics classes did not also lift weights outside the classes.

(C) On average, the volunteers who were assigned to the aerobics classes got more exercise in the months in which they took those classes than they had been getting before beginning the experiment.

(D) On average, the volunteers assigned to the aerobics classes found it less difficult to perform the mathematical calculation than did the volunteers assigned to the weight-training classes.

(E) On average, the volunteers assigned to the aerobics classes got a greater amount of aerobic exercise overall during the experiment, including any exercise outside the classes, than did the volunteers assigned to the weight-training classes.

22. Insurers and doctors are well aware that the incidence of lower-back injuries among office workers who spend long hours sitting is higher than that among people who regularly do physical work of a type known to place heavy stresses on the lower back. This shows that office equipment and furniture are not properly designed to promote workers' health.

Which one of the following, if true, most undermines the reasoning above?

(A) When they are at home, laborers and office workers tend to spend similar amounts of time sitting.

(B) Insurance companies tend to dislike selling policies to companies whose workers often claim to have back pain.

(C) People who regularly do physical work of a type known to place heavy stress on the lower back are encouraged to use techniques that reduce the degree of stress involved.

(D) Most of the lower-back injuries that office workers suffer occur while they are on the job.

(E) Consistent physical exercise is one of the most effective ways to prevent or recover from lower-back injuries.

23. Researchers have found that some unprotected areas outside of a national park that was designed to protect birds have substantially higher numbers of certain bird species than comparable areas inside the park.

Which one of the following, if true, most helps to explain the researchers' finding?

(A) Moose are much more prevalent inside the park, where hunting is prohibited, than outside the park, and moose eat much of the food that the birds need to survive.

(B) The researchers also found that some unprotected areas outside of the park have substantially higher numbers of certain reptile species than comparable areas inside the park.

(C) Researchers tagged a large number of birds inside the park; three months later some of these birds were recaptured outside the park.

(D) Both inside the park and just outside of it, there are riverside areas containing willows and other waterside growth that the bird species thrive on.

(E) The park was designed to protect endangered bird species, but some of the bird species that are present in higher numbers in the unprotected areas are also endangered.

GO ON TO THE NEXT PAGE.

24. A recent poll of a large number of households found that 47 percent of those with a cat had at least one person with a university degree, while 38 percent of households with a dog had at least one person with a university degree. Clearly, people who hold university degrees are more likely to live in a household with a cat than one with a dog.

The reasoning in the argument is flawed in that the argument

(A) ignores the possibility that a significant number of households might have both a cat and a dog

(B) takes for granted that there are not significantly more households with a dog than ones with a cat

(C) fails to consider how many of the households have at least one person without a university degree

(D) fails to consider to what extent people with university degrees participate in decisions about whether their households have a cat or dog

(E) ignores the possibility that two things can be correlated without being causally connected

25. Keeler wanted the institute to receive bad publicity. He and Greene were the only ones in a position to tell the press about the institute's potentially embarrassing affiliations, but Greene had no reason to do so. Therefore, it must have been Keeler who notified the press.

Which one of the following arguments is most closely parallel in its reasoning to the argument above?

(A) The only people who had any reason to write the anonymous letter were Johnson and Ringwold. Johnson and Ringwold both deny doing so. Ringwold, however, admits that she has written anonymous letters in the past. Thus, it must have been Ringwold who wrote the letter.

(B) Carter and Whitequill were the only ones who had any motive to bribe the public official. But Whitequill would have been too fearful that the bribery might somehow be made public. Carter, therefore, must be the person who bribed the public official.

(C) Other than Helms and Lapinski, no one had access to the equipment on Thursday, the day it was tampered with. Thus, since Helms had reason to tamper with the equipment and Lapinski did not, it must have been Helms who did it.

(D) When the bridge was designed, Fleming and Solano were the only ones capable of creating such a design. Fleming, however, had a strong reason to take credit for the design if it were his. Thus, since no one took credit for the design, it must have been the work of Solano.

(E) Cutter and Rengo are the only serious candidates for designing the new monument. Rengo has designed several beautiful monuments and has connections to the selection committee. Therefore, it will probably be Rengo who is awarded the job of designing the monument.

S T O P

IF YOU FINISH BEFORE TIME IS CALLED, YOU MAY CHECK YOUR WORK ON THIS SECTION ONLY.
DO NOT WORK ON ANY OTHER SECTION IN THE TEST.

SECTION IV

Time—35 minutes

23 Questions

<u>Directions</u>: Each set of questions in this section is based on a scenario with a set of conditions. The questions are to be answered on the basis of what can be logically inferred from the scenario and conditions. For each question, choose the response that most accurately and completely answers the question and mark that response on your answer sheet.

<u>Questions 1–6</u>

During a seven-week period, a department store will hold weekly sales on seven types of products—headphones, lamps, microwaves, printers, refrigerators, speakers, and televisions. Exactly one type of product will be on sale each week. The sale schedule will conform to the following constraints:

At least two weeks must separate the sale on headphones and the sale on speakers.

Printers and speakers must be on sale during consecutive weeks.

Televisions must be on sale during either the first or the seventh week.

If televisions are not on sale during the first week, refrigerators must be on sale then.

The sale on lamps must be in an earlier week than the sale on headphones.

1. The products scheduled for the last four sales, in order from the fourth sale to the seventh, could be

(A)   microwaves, lamps, speakers, printers
(B)   microwaves, printers, headphones, refrigerators
(C)   printers, microwaves, headphones, televisions
(D)   speakers, microwaves, televisions, headphones
(E)   speakers, printers, refrigerators, televisions

GO ON TO THE NEXT PAGE.

2. If the fourth sale is on printers, which one of the following must be true?

   (A)   The second sale is on lamps.
   (B)   The third sale is on speakers.
   (C)   The fifth sale is on microwaves.
   (D)   The sixth sale is on headphones.
   (E)   The seventh sale is on televisions.

3. If the fifth sale is on headphones, then the sale on microwaves could be earlier than the sale on

   (A)   headphones
   (B)   lamps
   (C)   printers
   (D)   refrigerators
   (E)   speakers

4. If refrigerators are on sale during the first week, then the order of the sales is completely determined if which one of the following is also true?

   (A)   The third sale is on headphones.
   (B)   The third sale is on speakers.
   (C)   The fourth sale is on lamps.
   (D)   The fourth sale is on microwaves.
   (E)   The sixth sale is on headphones.

5. If the sixth sale is on speakers, then the sale on microwaves must be later than the sale on

   (A)   headphones
   (B)   printers
   (C)   refrigerators
   (D)   speakers
   (E)   televisions

6. Which one of the following, if substituted for the constraint that if televisions are not on sale during the first week, refrigerators must be on sale then, would have the same effect in determining the order of the sales?

   (A)   Refrigerators must be on sale during either the first or the seventh week.
   (B)   If refrigerators are on sale during the first week, televisions must be on sale during the seventh week.
   (C)   If refrigerators are not on sale during the seventh week, televisions must be on sale then.
   (D)   If televisions are on sale during the first week, refrigerators cannot be on sale during the seventh week.
   (E)   If televisions are on sale during the seventh week, refrigerators must be on sale during the first week.

GO ON TO THE NEXT PAGE.

Questions 7–13

For an antiques fair at the local civic center, the fair's manager must assign each of six employees—Frank, Gladys, Hal, Keisha, Laura, and Mike—to one of three information booths—the organizers booth, the retailers booth, and the visitors booth. Each booth must be assigned at least one employee. The assignments are constrained as follows:

The retailers booth must have more employees than the visitors booth.

Neither Frank nor Keisha can be assigned to the visitors booth.

Neither Gladys nor Hal can be assigned to the organizers booth.

Gladys and Mike must work at the same booth as each other.

7. Which one of the following could be the assignment of employees to information booths?

(A) organizers booth: Keisha
retailers booth: Frank, Gladys, Laura, Mike
visitors booth: Hal

(B) organizers booth: Laura
retailers booth: Frank, Gladys, Keisha
visitors booth: Hal, Mike

(C) organizers booth: Frank, Keisha
retailers booth: Gladys, Mike
visitors booth: Hal, Laura

(D) organizers booth: Keisha, Laura
retailers booth: Gladys, Hal, Mike
visitors booth: Frank

(E) organizers booth: Frank, Hal, Keisha
retailers booth: Gladys, Mike
visitors booth: Laura

GO ON TO THE NEXT PAGE.

8. If neither Frank nor Keisha is assigned to the organizers booth, then which one of the following is a complete and accurate list of the booths to which Laura could be assigned?

(A) the organizers booth only
(B) the visitors booth only
(C) the organizers booth, the retailers booth
(D) the retailers booth, the visitors booth
(E) the organizers booth, the retailers booth, the visitors booth

9. If more employees are assigned to the organizers booth than to the retailers booth, then which one of the following employees must be assigned to the visitors booth?

(A) Mike
(B) Laura
(C) Keisha
(D) Hal
(E) Frank

10. Exactly how many of the employees are there any one of whom could be assigned to the organizers booth?

(A) one
(B) two
(C) three
(D) four
(E) five

11. If Hal is assigned to a booth with exactly one other employee, then which one of the following could be true?

(A) Laura is assigned to the organizers booth.
(B) Frank is assigned to the retailers booth.
(C) Hal is assigned to the retailers booth.
(D) Laura is assigned to the retailers booth.
(E) Gladys is assigned to the visitors booth.

12. If neither Hal nor Laura is assigned to the visitors booth, then which one of the following must be true?

(A) Frank and Laura are assigned to the organizers booth.
(B) Frank and Laura are assigned to the retailers booth.
(C) Gladys and Mike are assigned to the retailers booth.
(D) Gladys and Mike are assigned to the visitors booth.
(E) Hal and Laura are assigned to the retailers booth.

13. Which one of the following CANNOT be the group of employees assigned to the retailers booth?

(A) Frank, Gladys, Mike
(B) Frank, Hal, Keisha
(C) Frank, Hal, Laura
(D) Frank, Keisha, Laura
(E) Gladys, Laura, Mike

GO ON TO THE NEXT PAGE.

Questions 14–18

A textbook publishing company plans to publish six new textbooks, one in each of the following six subjects: linguistics, macroeconomics, psychology, Russian, statistics, and zoology. The company has three editors—Ferrer, Gupta, and Hendricks—available to edit the textbooks. Each editor must edit at least one textbook, and each textbook must be edited by exactly one editor. The following conditions apply to the assignment of editors to textbooks:

Ferrer must edit either the linguistics textbook or the zoology textbook, or both.

If Gupta edits the macroeconomics textbook, he cannot edit any other textbook.

Hendricks must edit exactly two textbooks.

Hendricks cannot edit the macroeconomics textbook.

The editor of the psychology textbook must also edit the statistics textbook.

14. Which one of the following could be a complete and accurate assignment of editors to the textbooks they edit?

(A)   Ferrer: macroeconomics, zoology
       Gupta: Russian, statistics
       Hendricks: linguistics, psychology
(B)   Ferrer: macroeconomics
       Gupta: psychology, statistics, zoology
       Hendricks: linguistics, Russian
(C)   Ferrer: linguistics, Russian
       Gupta: macroeconomics, zoology
       Hendricks: psychology, statistics
(D)   Ferrer: linguistics, psychology, statistics
       Gupta: zoology
       Hendricks: macroeconomics, Russian
(E)   Ferrer: linguistics, macroeconomics
       Gupta: psychology, statistics
       Hendricks: Russian, zoology

GO ON TO THE NEXT PAGE.

15. If the Russian textbook is edited by Hendricks, which one of the following could be true?

    (A) Ferrer edits the linguistics and zoology textbooks.
    (B) Ferrer edits the macroeconomics and zoology textbooks.
    (C) Gupta edits the linguistics textbook only.
    (D) Gupta edits the zoology textbook only.
    (E) Hendricks also edits the psychology textbook.

16. If the zoology textbook is edited by Gupta, which one of the following could be true?

    (A) Ferrer edits the psychology textbook.
    (B) Ferrer edits the Russian textbook.
    (C) Gupta also edits the macroeconomics textbook.
    (D) Hendricks edits the linguistics textbook.
    (E) Hendricks edits the Russian textbook.

17. If the linguistics textbook is edited by Hendricks, which one of the following must be true?

    (A) Ferrer edits the macroeconomics textbook.
    (B) Ferrer edits the statistics textbook.
    (C) Gupta edits the psychology textbook.
    (D) Hendricks also edits the Russian textbook.
    (E) Hendricks also edits the zoology textbook.

18. Which one of the following CANNOT be true?

    (A) Ferrer edits the linguistics, psychology, and statistics textbooks.
    (B) Ferrer edits the linguistics, Russian, and zoology textbooks.
    (C) Gupta edits the psychology, statistics, and Russian textbooks.
    (D) Hendricks edits the linguistics and Russian textbooks.
    (E) Hendricks edits the psychology and statistics textbooks.

GO ON TO THE NEXT PAGE.

Questions 19–23

An art gallery is scheduling five consecutive weeklong exhibitions, each featuring one of five local artists—Jackson, Katz, Lu, Norales, and Odede. During the opening reception for each exhibition, one of five musicians—Timmons, Vega, Wilson, Yoder, and Zheng—will perform. Each artist will have only one exhibition, and each musician will perform during only one opening reception. The schedule of artists and musicians must meet the following constraints:

 The Jackson exhibition is earlier than the Katz exhibition, which is earlier than the Lu exhibition.
 Timmons performs earlier than Vega, who performs earlier than Wilson.
 Wilson does not perform in the fourth week.
 Yoder does not perform at the Norales exhibition.
 Zheng performs at the Odede exhibition.

19. Which one of the following could be the schedule of artists and musicians from the first to the fifth week?

(A) Jackson and Timmons; Odede and Zheng; Katz and Vega; Norales and Wilson; Lu and Yoder

(B) Jackson and Yoder; Odede and Zheng; Norales and Timmons; Katz and Vega; Lu and Wilson

(C) Katz and Timmons; Odede and Zheng; Jackson and Vega; Lu and Yoder; Norales and Wilson

(D) Norales and Zheng; Odede and Yoder; Jackson and Timmons; Katz and Vega; Lu and Wilson

(E) Odede and Zheng; Jackson and Timmons; Katz and Vega; Norales and Yoder; Lu and Wilson

GO ON TO THE NEXT PAGE.

20. If Vega performs in the third week, which one of the following must be true?

 (A) Timmons performs in the first week.
 (B) Wilson performs in the fifth week.
 (C) Zheng performs in the fourth week.
 (D) The Katz exhibition is in the third week.
 (E) The Norales exhibition is in the second week.

21. If Timmons performs at the Jackson exhibition and Vega performs at the Katz exhibition, which one of the following could be true?

 (A) The Jackson exhibition is in the third week.
 (B) The Norales exhibition is in the fourth week.
 (C) Vega performs in the fourth week.
 (D) Yoder performs in the second week.
 (E) Zheng performs in the third week.

22. Which one of the following pairs is an artist and musician who CANNOT be scheduled for the same week as each other?

 (A) Jackson and Vega
 (B) Katz and Yoder
 (C) Lu and Timmons
 (D) Norales and Vega
 (E) Norales and Wilson

23. If Vega performs in an earlier week than the Katz exhibition, which one of the following must be true?

 (A) The Jackson exhibition is in an earlier week than Timmons's performance.
 (B) The Katz exhibition is in an earlier week than Yoder's performance.
 (C) The Lu exhibition is in an earlier week than Wilson's performance.
 (D) The Norales exhibition is in an earlier week than Yoder's performance.
 (E) The Odede exhibition is in an earlier week than Wilson's performance.

S T O P

IF YOU FINISH BEFORE TIME IS CALLED, YOU MAY CHECK YOUR WORK ON THIS SECTION ONLY.
DO NOT WORK ON ANY OTHER SECTION IN THE TEST.

Acknowledgment is made to the following sources from which material has been adapted for use in this test booklet:

Aaron Bernstein, "A Minimum-Wage Argument You Haven't Heard Before." ©1996 by the McGraw-Hill Companies.

William J. Broad, "Theory of Plate Movement Marks Zones That Breed Frequent Quakes." ©1995 by The New York Times.

Norbert Juergens, "The Biological Underpinnings of Namib Desert Fairy Circles" in *Science*. ©2013 by American Association for the Advancement of Science.

Mark D. Rosen, "Was *Shelley v. Kraemer* Incorrectly Decided? Some New Answers" in *California Law Review*. ©2007 by California Law Review, Inc.

William Speed Weed, "First to Ride." ©March 2002 by the Walt Disney Company.

Wait for the supervisor's instructions before you open the page to the topic.
Please print and sign your name and write the date in the designated spaces below.
Time: 35 Minutes

General Directions

You will have 35 minutes in which to plan and write an essay on the topic inside. Read the topic and the accompanying directions carefully. You will probably find it best to spend a few minutes considering the topic and organizing your thoughts before you begin writing. In your essay, be sure to develop your ideas fully, leaving time, if possible, to review what you have written. **Do not write on a topic other than the one specified. Writing on a topic of your own choice is not acceptable.**

No special knowledge is required or expected for this writing exercise. Law schools are interested in the reasoning, clarity, organization, language usage, and writing mechanics displayed in your essay. How well you write is more important than how much you write.

Confine your essay to the blocked, lined area on the front and back of the separate Writing Sample Response Sheet. Only that area will be reproduced for law schools. Be sure that your writing is legible.

Both this topic sheet and your response sheet must be turned in to the testing staff before you leave the room.

Topic Code	Print Your Full Name Here		
164299	Last	First	M.I.

Date	Sign Your Name Here
/ /	

Scratch Paper
Do not write your essay in this space.

LSAT® Writing Sample Topic

<u>Directions</u>: The scenario presented below describes two choices, either one of which can be supported on the basis of the information given. Your essay should consider both choices and argue for one over the other, based on the two specified criteria and the facts provided. There is no "right" or "wrong" choice: a reasonable argument can be made for either.

A farmer is deciding between two five-year contracts. One would require using the farm's fields exclusively to produce corn; the other would require using the fields exclusively to produce soybean. Using the facts below, write an essay in which you argue for one choice over the other based on the following two criteria:

- The farmer wants to minimize the effort required to raise and harvest the farm's crops.
- The farmer wants to manage the farm's land in a sustainable and environmentally conscious way.

Corn typically yields significantly more usable produce per acre than soybean does. Corn typically requires more water than soybean does. Neither plant can grow without the presence of nitrogen in the soil. Corn does not produce nitrogen, which necessitates the use of fertilizer in the fields. As it grows, corn absorbs from the atmosphere a large amount of carbon dioxide (CO_2), a greenhouse gas. Corn produces large amounts of unusable plant material that releases half of the absorbed CO_2 back into the atmosphere when it eventually decays. Corn's roots compact the soil in such a way that it reduces the erosion of topsoil. In order to plant corn on the same land several years in a row, a farmer must replace nutrients in the soil before replanting.

Soybean plants produce their own nitrogen. Soybean roots do not protect the topsoil from erosion. The farmer owns a combine for harvesting, but only owns the attachment for harvesting corn. A different attachment is needed to harvest soybeans. Soybean plants are naturally more resistant to pests and disease than corn plants are. Soybean can be cultivated on the same land for several years in a row without depleting the soil of nutrients. Soybean captures little atmospheric CO_2 as it grows, and leaves relatively little unusable plant material behind after harvesting.

WPAC164A

Scratch Paper
Do not write your essay in this space.

COMPUTING YOUR SCORE

Directions:

1. Use the Answer Key on the next page to check your answers.

2. Use the Scoring Worksheet below to compute your raw score.

3. Use the Score Conversion Chart to convert your raw score into the 120–180 scale.

Scoring Worksheet

1. Enter the number of questions you answered correctly in each section.

	Number Correct
SECTION I.................	_____
SECTION II................	_____
SECTION III..............	_____
SECTION IV	_____

2. Enter the sum here: _____
   This is your Raw Score.

Conversion Chart
For Converting Raw Score to the 120–180 LSAT Scaled Score
LSAT Form 8LSN130

Reported Score	Raw Score Lowest	Raw Score Highest
180	99	101
179	98	98
178	97	97
177	*	*
176	96	96
175	95	95
174	94	94
173	93	93
172	92	92
171	91	91
170	90	90
169	89	89
168	87	88
167	86	86
166	85	85
165	83	84
164	82	82
163	80	81
162	78	79
161	77	77
160	75	76
159	73	74
158	71	72
157	69	70
156	68	68
155	66	67
154	64	65
153	62	63
152	60	61
151	59	59
150	57	58
149	55	56
148	53	54
147	51	52
146	50	50
145	48	49
144	46	47
143	45	45
142	43	44
141	41	42
140	40	40
139	38	39
138	37	37
137	35	36
136	34	34
135	32	33
134	31	31
133	30	30
132	29	29
131	28	28
130	26	27
129	25	25
128	24	24
127	23	23
126	22	22
125	*	*
124	21	21
123	20	20
122	19	19
121	18	18
120	0	17

*There is no raw score that will produce this scaled score for this form.

ANSWER KEY

SECTION I

1.	A	8.	B	15.	D	22.	B
2.	B	9.	E	16.	C	23.	D
3.	E	10.	C	17.	E	24.	C
4.	C	11.	D	18.	D	25.	E
5.	B	12.	A	19.	A	26.	C
6.	D	13.	D	20.	E	27.	E
7.	C	14.	A	21.	B		

SECTION II

1.	A	8.	C	15.	E	22.	B
2.	B	9.	A	16.	A	23.	C
3.	D	10.	A	17.	C	24.	A
4.	C	11.	D	18.	A	25.	D
5.	B	12.	B	19.	B	26.	D
6.	B	13.	E	20.	B		
7.	E	14.	C	21.	A		

SECTION III

1.	B	8.	A	15.	C	22.	E
2.	A	9.	C	16.	E	23.	A
3.	B	10.	C	17.	C	24.	B
4.	B	11.	C	18.	E	25.	C
5.	D	12.	B	19.	E		
6.	A	13.	A	20.	D		
7.	E	14.	D	21.	E		

SECTION IV

1.	C	8.	A	15.	B	22.	C
2.	B	9.	D	16.	B	23.	D
3.	D	10.	C	17.	D		
4.	A	11.	B	18.	C		
5.	A	12.	D	19.	B		
6.	E	13.	D	20.	B		
7.	A	14.	E	21.	E		

LSAT® PREP TOOLS

The Official LSAT SuperPrep II™

SuperPrep II contains everything you need to prepare for the LSAT—a guide to all three LSAT question types, three actual LSATs, explanations for all questions in the three practice tests, answer keys, writing samples, and score-conversion tables, plus invaluable test-taking instructions to help with pacing and timing. SuperPrep has long been our most comprehensive LSAT preparation book, and SuperPrep II is even better. The practice tests in SuperPrep II are PrepTest 62 (December 2010 LSAT), PrepTest 63 (June 2011 LSAT), and one test that has never before been disclosed.

With this book you can

• Practice on genuine LSAT questions

• Review explanations for right and wrong answers

• Target specific categories for intensive review

• Simulate actual LSAT conditions

LSAC sets the standard for LSAT prep—and SuperPrep II raises the bar!

Available at your favorite bookseller.

LSAC.org